michi
Japanese Arts and Ways

From *chado*—"the Way of tea"—to *budo*—"the martial Way"—Japan has succeeded in spiritualizing a number of classical arts. The names of these skills often end in Do, also pronounced Michi, meaning the "Way." By studying a Way in detail, we discover vital principles that transcend the art and relate more broadly to the art of living itself. Featuring the work of H. E. Davey and other select authors, books in the series MICHI: JAPANESE ARTS AND WAYS focus on these Do forms. They are about discipline and spirituality, about moving from the particular to the universal . . . to benefit people of any culture.

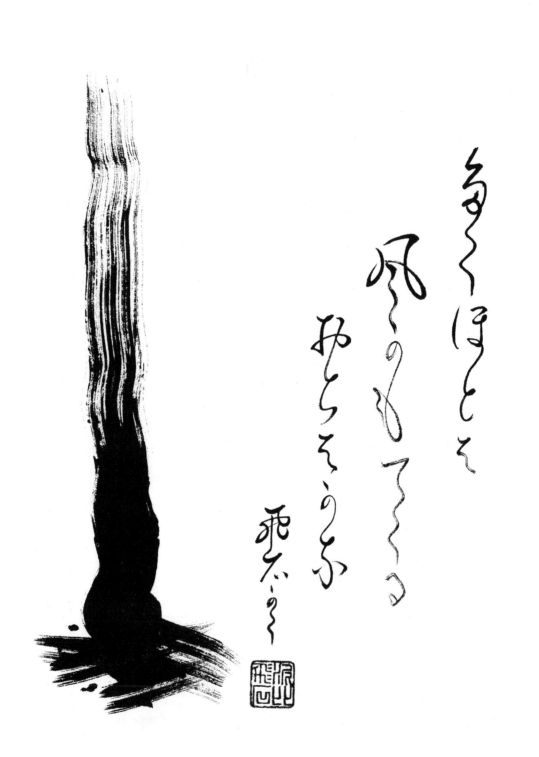

Brush Meditation

A Japanese
Way to
Mind & Body
Harmony

H. E. Davey

Michi: Japanese Arts and Ways

Stone Bridge Press • Berkeley, California

Michi: Japanese Arts and Ways, volume 1. Series supervisor: H. E. Davey.

Published by Stone Bridge Press, P. O. Box 8208, Berkeley, CA 94707

TEL 510-524-8732 • sbp@stonebridge.com • www.stonebridge.com

FRONTISPIECE: Painting of bonfire and poem by H. E. Davey.

Some of the artwork reproduced in this book has previously appeared in the following publications: "Ki" in *Furyu* (Spring–Summer 1995); "Mushin" in *Nichi Bei Times* (January 1, 1998); "Fudoshin" in *Hokubei Mainichi* (January 1, 1997).

Cover title lettering, cover design, and interior layout by L. J. C. Shimoda.

Photography by Ann Kameoka.

All artwork by the author, except the bonfire and poem on page 133 by Ohsaki Jun.

Text, calligraphy, and photographs © 1999 H. E. Davey.

Printed in the United States of America.

10 9 8 7 6 5 4 3 2   2005 2004 2003 2002 2001 2000

LIBRARY OF CONGRESS CATALOGING-IN-PUBLICATION DATA
Davey, H. E.
    Brush meditation: a Japanese way to mind & body harmony / H. E. Davey.
        p. cm.
    Includes bibliographical references.
    ISBN 1-880656-38-8
    1. Calligraphy, Japanese. 2. Aesthetics, Japanese. 3. Art therapy. 4. Mind and
body. I. Title.
ND1457.J33D38   1999
745.6'1'0952—dc21   99-26561
                                                                           CIP

CONTENTS

PREFACE

We are witnessing the meeting of East and West. Through positive, nonbiased Eastern and Western cultural exchange, a new, more balanced, more enlightened global culture may result. While I explore calligraphic painting (shodo) as well as other Japanese cultural arts in *Brush Meditation*, and examine the meditative aspects of shodo and various Japanese arts, one of the main reasons I wrote this book is to let other Westerners know that it is possible, and meaningful, for non-Japanese to participate in traditional Japanese art forms.

At their deepest levels, the martial arts (budo), tea ceremony (chado), flower arrangement (kado), calligraphy, and other Japanese arts are the same. Despite their obvious physical differences, these arts share a common set of aesthetics and, more importantly, they require the acquisition of identical positive character traits if you are to become successful in their performance.

Note that many of these arts end in the word *do*. "Do" means "the way," and it indicates that a given activity has transcended its utilitarian function, that this action has been elevated to the level of art, and that its proponents are teaching it as a way of life. A "do" form is an art that allows you to grasp the ultimate nature of the whole of life by examining yourself in great detail through a singular aspect of life: to grasp the universal through the particular.

Many artistic principles and important mental states are universal for the various Japanese "ways." One of the most significant and basic principles that these arts share is the concept of mind and body coordination. Few of us are required to use a brush in daily life, but most of us are interested in realizing our full potential and enhancing our mental state as well as our physical health. Because integrating the mind and body allows us to achieve these goals, the relationship between the mind and body, along with how to achieve a state of mind-body harmony, is one of the main themes of this book.

Some painters make statements to the effect that "if the mind is correct, the brush is correct." In Japanese swordsmanship, it is not uncommon to speak of a unity of mind, body, and sword. Likewise, in Zen meditation, students are encouraged to arrive at a state of mind and body coordination, a state of self-harmony. All of these assertions point to the necessity of integrating the mind and body in action. Mental and physical harmony is also vital for realizing our full potential in daily living, and it remains one of the central elements needed for mastery of any of the classical Japanese ways.

Yet, perhaps surprisingly, although I serve as Director of the Sennin Foundation Center for Japanese Cultural Arts, I'm not teaching and pursuing the above-mentioned art forms because of an overwhelming interest in Japanese culture. While I certainly am, of course, interested in Japan, my main intention in studying these arts is to examine the nature of the self, the universe, and life as a whole. This point is vital, as the miscellaneous "do" all indicate a "way" that transcends boundaries and limitations. It is in the end not a "Japanese way," but rather a human way and, ultimately, the way of the universe.

In *Brush Meditation*, shodo, or Japanese brush writing, will be used as a representative example of how the various "do" forms help us discover principles that relate universally to all aspects of living and that can enhance our lives. The book begins with a brief history of calligraphy and painting in Asia and explains why these arts hold relevance for the West. Following this is an explanation of mind-body unification in shodo and painting, as well as the basic techniques of controlling the brush. The aesthetics and principles that are universal for the Japanese cultural arts are also explored, along with their importance for cultivating calmness and concentration. Of course, a few introductory lessons in brush meditation, calligraphy, and painting are included so that you can work with the brush and begin to experience for yourself the mind-body connection. Sources for shodo and painting supplies are at the back of the book.

Shodo mastery takes years of practice, and formal instruction with a teacher, so your goal in using this book should primarily be one of exploration and discovery. Instead of worrying about the formally "correct" ways of drawing lines with a brush, for now you should concentrate on experiencing how movement, everyday life, and the spirit are inextricably linked.

I am not a master of any of the Japanese artistic disciplines. Still, in both the United States and Japan, I have had unique opportunities to study some of the Japanese arts that remain inaccessible to many people in the West. It is my wish to share with interested others a bit of what I have been able to absorb about these art forms. *Brush Meditation: A Japanese Way to Mind & Body Harmony* amounts to an act of personal study, self-examination, and analysis that I hope will also be relevant to other people interested in art, meditation, and Japanese culture.

ABOUT THE CALLIGRAPHY IN THIS BOOK

Compared to some methods of Japanese calligraphy, my teacher Kobara Ranseki's system of shodo follows the original Chinese version closely and is fairly conservative in approach. The inspiration for Kobara Sensei's methodology can be traced to his late teacher Fuku-zawa Seiran Sensei as well as to the famed Chinese calligraphers Ogishi and Chiei. Mr. Kobara's artistic style features a precise execution of form. This is combined with characters that are dynamic, yet exceed-ingly smooth and elegant. Unlike the sharp corners and hard edges encountered in some forms of shodo, Kobara Ranseki Sensei's flowing system utilizes a natural and more rounded execution (similar to that found in Chiei's ancient calligraphy classic *Sen-Ji-Mon*). This relaxed, fluid, and graceful approach can even be detected in his *kaisho* (printed style) characters.

The calligraphy in this book reflects Kobara Sensei's influence. The large pieces scattered throughout have been provided to illustrate different styles of shodo and to serve as places to pause and reflect. I hope they will also inspire you to pursue formal instruction in brush writing.

ACKNOWLEDGMENTS

Brush Meditation: A Japanese Way to Mind & Body Harmony is ded-icated to my teacher, Kobara Ranseki Sensei. Since 1986 Kobara Sensei has taught me the art of shodo. But more than this, he has served as a continual source of encouragement, communicated as much by his positive, kind, and gentle presence as through his direct words and actions. Kobara Sensei has been instrumental in showing me a way of

teaching and uplifting others that transcends verbal communication
. . . a rare art indeed.

As a child, I began to study Shin-shin-toitsu-do, a system of Japanese yoga based on the principles of mind and body integration, and
this has been an invaluable aid in my understanding of shodo as well as
Japanese ink painting. I would like to acknowledge my debt to my
teachers of Shin-shin-toitsu-do, particularly Hashimoto Tetsuichi Sensei, who is a certified teacher with the Tempu-kai of Tokyo. While
many founders of the Japanese arts mastered coordination of mind and
body, Nakamura Tempu Sensei, originator of Shin-shin-toitsu-do, is an
outstanding example of this mastery. After a number of years studying
a wide diversity of spiritual disciplines, he achieved satori (realization)
while living in the Himalayas. He returned to Japan from India in 1919,
where he founded Shin-shin-toitsu-do: "the Way of Mind and Body
Unification." Coinciding with this, he began to spontaneously produce
works of calligraphic art in a unique and unprecedented style. Paintings, sculptures, and ceramic ware sprang from the same source of
inspiration. According to Nakamura Sensei, this source was the essential unity of mind and body; if the mind could conceive or perceive
something, the body could accurately create it—as long as no gap existed between the mind and body. This philosophy echoed sentiments
held by the forefathers of most Japanese cultural arts, and it describes in
a nutshell one of the primary aspects of personal development found in
the Japanese art forms.

The idea of art as a tangible expression of mind has had great
appeal to me for some time. The traditional belief in Japan is that one's
personality is revealed in calligraphy. Leaders in any of the Japanese cultural disciplines were expected to be able to execute fine script. (When

some of my teachers of various arts would visit, they would often offer their brush writing as gifts.) This fact, combined with a lifelong exposure to Japanese culture, my experiences in studying the arts of Japan, including Japanese yoga, and a wish to further my understanding of "the way" led me to pursue shodo and, ultimately, to write this book. Shin-shin-toitsu-do has greatly influenced the manner in which I teach shodo, and many of the concepts in this book are based on my experiences studying Japanese yoga.

I'd also like to acknowledge my mother, Elaine Davey, now over eighty years old, and my late father, Victor H. Davey, both of whom encouraged my childhood interest in art and music. What little artistic ability I possess is, at least partially, inherited from my dad, who was a talented watercolor painter and cartoonist.

Ann Harue Kameoka, my wife, helped with the editing and photography. She deserves a great deal of credit for putting up with my artist's temperament as well as for supporting my involvement in shodo and other Japanese cultural arts. Without her support and understanding, many of my accomplishments in these arts would have been much more difficult to attain.

Ohsaki Jun, my student of several years, posed for many of the illustrations. He was also helpful in checking my translation of Japanese texts and terms.

Finally, this book would not exist in its present form if my student Linda Shimoda had not introduced me to Stone Bridge Press. My thanks go out to Linda as well as to Peter Goodman and everyone at Stone Bridge Press.

H. E. DAVEY
Richmond, California

A NOTE ON THE JAPANESE LANGUAGE

Shodo is, obviously, intimately tied to the Japanese language. Japanese is the universal language of all the Japanese "do," or "way" forms. For example, in judo competitions throughout the world, the referee gives all commands in Japanese.

A single expression in Japanese can communicate several different shades of significance in a way that an individual term in English cannot. For instance, the Japanese word *kokoro* can alternately express "mind," "spirit," "soul," "heart," and even hint at "emotion" or "feeling." For this reason alone, it is often preferable to use the native Japanese terminology in the various Japanese arts rather than attempt an English equivalent.

Japan's arts of painting and calligraphy are not merely graphic skills; they are truly Japanese cultural arts and spiritual paths. A modest comprehension of the Japanese language can open certain doors, leading to a deeper awareness of Japan's culture and making the practice of the country's cultural activities more profound. This understanding also allows the Western fine arts devotee to more easily interact with both Japanese authorities and genuine Western experts, many of whom have spent time studying in Japan, without fear of embarrassment.

To read the Japanese words in this book and sidestep chagrin over garbled Japanese terms, merely follow the guidelines below.

a is pronounced "ah" as in father
e is pronounced "eh" as in Edward
i is pronounced "ee" as in police
o is pronounced "oh" as in oats
u is pronounced "oo" as in tune

Double consonants are spoken with a brief break between syllables. In Japanese, *r* is pronounced as a mix of the English *r* and *l*. The special orthographic signs called macrons, used in some books to indicate extended vowel sounds in Japanese, are not used here.

When talking or writing in Japanese, it is customary to place the family (last) name first and the given (first) name second. This convention has, with one or two exceptions, been observed in *Brush Meditation*. In some cases, the Japanese pronunciations of Chinese words and proper names are used, as are "non-standard" romanized spellings of common or well-established Japanese names. *Sensei*, a Japanese appellation of respect that means "teacher," is invariably placed after a professor's family name. It is used in an identical manner to the honorific suffix *-san*.

KI
Life Energy
Kaisho

Chapter 1

THE LANGUAGE
OF SHODO

Shodo, or the "way of calligraphy," has been one of the most highly respected arts in Japan for centuries. It is currently studied by an exceedingly large segment of Japanese society; everyone from executives to housewives seems to be involved in the practice of this ancient art. Surprisingly, shodo has received relatively little exposure in the West, but in recent years it is finally showing some signs of gaining recognition abroad.

The Origins of Shodo and Ink Painting

The Japanese written language is derived from ancient Chinese written symbols adopted by the Japanese around the fifth century. According to oral tradition, Chinese characters were born around 2700 B.C., the creation of an enigmatic man with four eyes called Tsangh-hsieh, who is said to have been captivated by the footprints of beasts and birds. The God of Heaven was believed to have been so moved by Tsangh-hsieh's ingenious bird-based characters that he made grain drop from the clouds as a symbol of his happiness with humankind.

Archaeologists have found uncomplicated drawings engraved on pieces of tortoiseshell and oracle bone dating from the Shang period in China (1766–1122 B.C.). These pictures on bone and shell were the archetypes of future Chinese characters. Ancient Chinese shamans would bore holes in the shells and/or bones, which were then placed in a sacred fire. The surfaces of these objects would crack and split, and the resulting fissures would be deciphered by the priests, who etched their impressions of the Voice of Heaven on the bone or shell in the form of simple sketches. (To this day, Chinese characters retain overtones of reverence and magic.) Eventually these pictographs were utilized for legal transactions, which were conducted via the exchange of etched strips of bamboo or wood. Later in China, these writings came into religious and official usage as bell inscriptions.

The Evolution of Script Styles

A nonstandardized system of script, known as *daiten*,* or the "great seal script," developed from these bell inscriptions. Following this, a number of script systems were created by a variety of people and accepted by the government of the time for official use. During the Ch'in period (221–206 B.C.), Li Ssu altered the great seal script to make it simpler. His creation was called *shoten*, or the "small seal script." Shoten characters were uniform in size and widely taught in ancient schools as a means of attempting to tie together the many different lan-

---

* Here and elsewhere, in keeping with the convention of Japanese cultural arts, script styles and art forms that may have originated in China but that have been adopted by the Japanese are identified by their Japanese, not Chinese, names.

guages spoken across China. Also during the Ch'in period, China saw the introduction of silk surfaces for writing, ink sticks, and brushes. All of this made the characters easier still to write. Li Ssu is believed to have created only three thousand characters, but over ten thousand were being used by A.D. 200. About the same time, *korei* ("ancient scribe's script") was introduced by Ch'eng Mo. He straightened curved lines and made squares more circular. This made the symbols easier to draw and more pleasing to look at.

During the Han dynasty (206 B.C.–A.D. 220) the philosophy of Confucius became the official doctrine of China. During this same era, the Chinese invented paper, which allowed them to reproduce Confucian teachings by hand. Also during the Han dynasty *kan-reisho*, a variant of the scribe's script, was created, and it was from this that printed-style characters *(kaisho)* and semicursive-style writing *(gyosho)* were developed. *Sosho*, which is a fully cursive script, was not an even more abbreviated version of kaisho and gyosho, despite what is often believed. Sosho was, rather, an independent development of the cursive versions of the earlier seal script. (This is why there is not necessarily a strict correlation between the semicursive and cursive versions of the same character.)

Chinese Calligraphy in Japan

During the Asuka (A.D. 552–645) and Early Nara to Nara (A.D. 645–94) periods in Japan, many different elements of Chinese culture, including Chinese characters, came to this island nation. Initially the Japanese used the entire multitude of Chinese scripts, embracing quite a few of the Chinese readings while adding just as many of their own.

Eventually, characters were modified in Japan, and three new scripts were born: *man'yo-gana*, *hiragana*, and *katakana*.

During the fifth to tenth centuries in Japan, man'yo-gana (also called *hentaigana*) was developed as a sort of phonetic Japanese alphabet. That is, it did not make use of the actual meanings of the Chinese characters upon which it was based but used forms based on those characters to represent the syllables of the Japanese language. To arrive at a more standard written usage, sosho (cursive) man'yo-gana, which has many variants, was simplified and organized into the script known as hiragana. Hiragana is the primary phonetic script used in Japan today. Consisting of forty-six characters, its forms were finally standardized only in the past hundred years. Another phonetic script, the more angular katakana, was developed from kaisho using forms extracted from parts of Chinese characters. For more about hiragana and katakana, see pages 26–27.

Classical Japanese calligraphy should not be thought of as mere penmanship. Considering that Chinese characters began as simplified drawings, it is evident that no clear-cut dividing line can be found between drawing, ink painting, and calligraphy.

Hiragana and sosho man'yo-gana possess a soft, rounded appearance and were thought at the time to be more suitable for women. (In the eighth century, the famed poetry anthology *Man'yo-shu* was written by a woman using man'yo-gana.) The printed-style kaisho and semicursive gyosho were believed to be more suitable for men and were used for administrative and religious purposes during the same period. In China a distinction was never made between the writing of men and women. Modern Japan also no longer preserves this distinction.

Even though the spoken languages and cultures of Japan and China differ greatly, they share a common set of Asian characters. Note, however, that while these characters are used to form a system of written communication, classical Japanese calligraphy should not be thought of as mere penmanship. Considering that Chinese characters began as simplified drawings, it is evident that no clear-cut dividing line can be found between drawing, ink painting *(suiboku-e* or *sumi-e)*, and calligraphy. In the Japanese language, the word *sho* (which is also pronounced *kaku*) can mean either "to write," "to draw," or "to paint." Likewise, the title *kakite* can be used to denote either a painter or a calligrapher. Even linguistically, a clear differentiation is not always made in Japan between painting and brush writing. To quote Yanagida Taiun Sensei, one of Japan's most well-respected artists and calligraphers:

> Sho (Japanese calligraphy) as we see it in Asia is an art that was created at the same time as and has developed along with the art of painting. But from the moment of creation, sho led a separate existence with abstract characters, as opposed to painting with specific images. Although the artistic value of each was the same until the present, these two media used absolutely different modes of expression. Sho has two functions: like the European alphabet it serves as a means of communication and like it is an expression of beauty. This led naturally to the development of expressing and drawing poetry and prose in an artistic manner. That is why in the East there is conviction about the aesthetic unity of painting and calligraphy. [1]

Shodo and ink painting cannot be separated from their historical and cultural matrix, which is why I've prefaced the painting exercises in this book with this historical section. Shodo is based on uncommonly elusive and elegant artistic skills, which are in turn based on technical and mental principles. While shodo's psychophysical concepts are universal in character, these principles developed from, and were affected by, their disseminators' modes of thinking, which were an immediate outgrowth of Japan's religions, arts, aesthetics, and history. (*Wabi, sabi,* and some of the more important Japanese aesthetic and philosophical ideals that influenced the development and style of shodo are explored later in this chapter.) Without at least some comprehension of Japan's historical and cultural matrix and some understanding of the esoteric principles that make up shodo, one's capacity to paint suffers.

Of course, shodo, at its deepest levels, goes beyond societal boundaries. Nevertheless, when avowing the art's unrestricted and universal aspects that transcend culture, you should not go to the opposite extreme of disregarding shodo's abundant elements that are an outgrowth of Japanese culture. Without these cultural characteristics that make up the structure of the art, your study is one-dimensional. A better approach is to observe that the most profound principles of shodo are universal—counterparts can be detected in many non-Japanese disciplines—while at the same time appreciating the ample Japanese components that give shodo its discernible framework.

I hope that this brief portrayal of shodo history will encourage you to more thoroughly explore the art's ties to Japan by practicing different Japanese cultural arts such as flower arrangement, Shin-shin-toitsu-do (Japanese yoga), and others—all of which have a much closer connection to shodo than you might think.

Moving beyond Writing

The *kanji*, or written characters, used in both Japan and China have transcended their utilitarian function and collectively serve as a visually stirring piece of fine art. Shodo allows the dynamic movement of the artist's *ki* ("life energy" or "spirit") to become observable in the form of rich black ink. In great examples of shodo, you can sense both the rhythm of music as well as the smooth, elegant, and balanced construction of refined architecture. Many practitioners of this art feel that the visible rhythm of Japanese calligraphy ultimately embodies a "picture of the mind"—and accomplished calligraphers recognize that it actually discloses your spiritual state. This recognition is concisely summed up by the traditional Japanese saying:

> *Kokoro tadashikereba sunawachi fude tadashii.*
> If your mind is correct, the brush will be correct.

Some Japanese calligraphers and psychologists have written books on the examination of an individual's personality through calligraphy. Just as certain American and European companies have employed handwriting analysts to help them select the best individuals for executive posts, the Japanese for hundreds of years have expected their leaders in any field to display fine, composed script. (Recently this expectation has faded due to the advent of word processors.)

It is even said that health defects can be revealed in the appearance of *byohitsu*, or "sick strokes." This stems from the belief that brush strokes reveal the state of the body and subconscious mind—including its strengths and weaknesses—at the moment the brush is put to paper. People believed that the subconscious could be influenced in a positive manner by studying and copying consummate examples of calligraphy by extraordinary individuals; by doing so you could cultivate a strength of character akin to that of the artist being copied. Even today, some of Japan's highest executives and politicians endeavor to develop the necessary traits for success by reproducing the artwork of an emperor or famous religious leader.

Since shodo is considered an art form, you do not need to be able to read Chinese characters, or the Japanese phonetic scripts of hiragana or katakana, to admire its dynamic beauty. Within Japanese calligraphy, you find the essential elements that constitute all art: creativity, balance, rhythm, grace, and the beauty of line. These aspects of shodo can be recognized and appreciated by every culture.

Kanji and Kana

Most languages, including English, use a limited assemblage of phonetic symbols to represent the sounds making up individual words in written configuration. Japanese and Chinese, on the other hand, use pictographs to represent words or concepts, as well as thousands of ideographs, each of which has a particular meaning. This system contains a vast number of symbols, thus adding tremendous variety to Japanese calligraphy, and thereby producing a potentially infinite combination of expressions. Many kanji (Chinese characters) are literally abstracted and abbreviated pictures (as opposed to letters) that can stir emotion in the observer, as some paintings do, because of their depth and diversity. Figure 1 shows the graphic evolution of the character for "mountain" from its ancient "picture state" to the modern character. Figure 2 shows the same elaboration of the symbol for "paintbrush." A

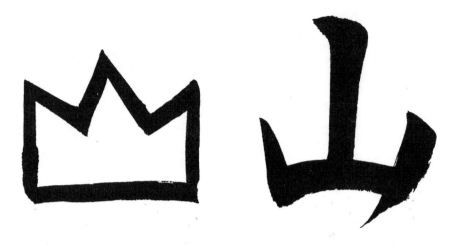

FIG. 1. The graphic evolution of the character for "mountain" from its ancient "picture state" to the modern character.

hand holding a brush can easily be seen in the ancient character. To even the most casual observer, it should be clear that many characters are truly pictures, and for this reason the calligrapher paints or draws these characters as much as writes them.

Chinese characters can be divided into four categories: pictographs, ideographs, semantic composites, and phonetic-semantic composites. Pictographs started out as prehistoric images of natural phenomena and everyday objects. Ideographs are symbols, while pictographs amount to concrete signs. (For example, the ideograph for "above" was first written as a dot over a horizontal line.) When ideographs and pictographs were combined, semantic composites were formed by linking more than one existing character. (The semantic composite for "bright" is a fusion of the kanji for "sun" and the character for "moon." Both of these natural objects provide "bright" light.) A phonetic-semantic composite links a semantic element with a phonetic

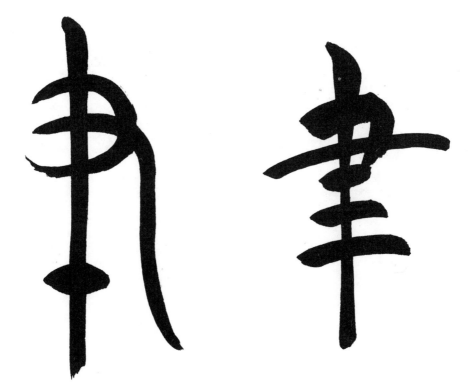

FIG. 2. The graphic evolution of the character for "paintbrush" from its ancient "picture state" to the modern character.

element; this sort of symbol will, therefore, take its actual meaning from one of its aspects and its pronunciation from another.

Each character can also be written in several different styles, which increases their creative potential. Kaisho (printed style), gyosho (semi-cursive style), and sosho (cursive style)—see page 17—are the most common variants. To illustrate these three basic scripts, the character *do* (also pronounced *michi*), which means "the way" in a spiritual sense, is presented in kaisho, gyosho, and sosho forms in Figures 3–5.

FIG. 3. The character *do* painted in kaisho (printed style).

FIG. 4. The character *do* painted in gyosho (semicursive style).

FIG. 5. The character *do* painted in sosho (cursive style).

Other more exotic methods, such as the aforementioned seal scripts and ancient scribe's script, exist as well.

As previously noted on pages 17–18, not too long after the Japanese adopted Chinese characters, around the sixth century A.D., they also originated two native systems of phonetic writing, hiragana and katakana. Both kana systems are syllabaries. That is, they are used to write all the sounds of the Japanese language. All modern Japanese texts are written in a mix of kanji and kana. In a Japanese newspaper, for instance, you will see a combination of kanji and hiragana with a sprinkling of katakana. (In principle, Japanese could be written with kana syllables alone—as many children's books are— but this would eliminate the meanings conveyed by the kanji and, because of the many Japanese homonyms, make the written text very hard to comprehend.)

Hiragana and katakana characters represent the same forty-six syl-

FIG. 6. The katakana version of the sylla-
ble *ro* is an extracted element of the character at right.

FIG. 7. The hiragana version of the syl-
lable *ro* is a simplified form of the character at right.

lables in Japanese texts, but they have different origins and are used in
different ways.

Katakana characters are merely a single component of a kanji
(Chinese character) that has sometimes been extracted or simplified.
Katakana tend to be somewhat square and angular in appearance and
are used for writing words borrowed into Japanese from foreign languages, for some scientific terms, and for emphasis. Figure 6 shows the
katakana *ro* and the character from which it is derived.

Hiragana characters are an abbreviation and simplification of
whole kanji forms and have a more rounded, flowing, and graceful
demeanor than katakana. Hiragana is used to record grammatical
inflections in adjectives, adverbs, and verbs and for words no longer
written in kanji. Figure 7 illustrates the hiragana version of *ro* and its
accompanying related kanji.

Since this book is designed primarily as an introduction to the cultural, artistic, and meditative aspects of Japanese calligraphy and painting, it does not include a complete list of kanji, katakana, and hiragana. However, any serious student of shodo should own a comprehensive Japanese dictionary, which should also explain the order of brush strokes used in each Japanese symbol. *The New Nelson Japanese-English Dictionary* (Tokyo and Boston: Tuttle Publishing, 1997), a revised edition of the classic work, is an excellent resource.

Few people are aware that many of the fundamental brush strokes in shodo are similar to or the same as the strokes employed in classical Asian ink painting. You use essentially the same sort of brush, ink stick, ink stone, and paper in both arts. Skilled calligraphers can produce simple yet quite respectable ink drawings merely by relying upon their experience in shodo, and the two related arts are not infrequently combined to form a single composition.

Universal Principles in Japanese Art

Certain philosophical and artistic ideals are universal and apply to all methods of Japanese art. From the martial arts to Japan's fine arts to the traditional tea ceremony, particular aesthetic codes are historically held in common. Shodo and sumi-e are no exception to this rule.

Among the most significant artistic ideas in Japan are the concepts of wabi, sabi, *shibumi,* and *shibui.* These aesthetic ideals, and others, have had a profound influence on the evolution of Japanese calligraphy. I believe that if you do not understand these aesthetic principles, no great appreciation of any Japanese cultural art, whether it be shodo or *shakuhachi* flute, is possible.

28

WABI AND SABI

"Wabi" actually means "poverty." This has no negative implications but hints at the innocent contentment that can be found when you listen to a gentle springtime rain tap-tapping on the roof of a simple cabin. Wabi is outside of intellectual complexity and all forms of self-importance and artificiality; it relates to the discovery of the simple truths of nature. Just as nature is asymmetrical, irregular, and imperfect, wabi is the flawlessness of natural imperfection. Asymmetrical balance is vital in shodo:

> Every time I teach, I explain that art is balance. This
> principle can be understood throughout the world.
> —Kobara Ranseki Sensei

Also important is the understanding of when to use light or dark versus heavy or light lines of ink. When writing *waka* (a form of poetry), the placement of every stanza, or line of characters, in relationship to every other line on the paper is crucial. All the lines must form a balanced and artistically correct design as a whole. Kobara Ranseki teaches that "unbalance of balance" is beautiful in Japanese art.

In a way, wabi is the elegance of artlessness and even ugliness. When this artless, imperfect beauty is coupled with a particular uncultured antiquity, or even the illusion of this aged attribute, Japanese artists employ the word "sabi" to describe it. "Sabi" is literally "solitude" or "lonesomeness," but in specific instances it can also suggest an effortless quality. (Like wabi, it is almost impossible to describe directly. It can only be truly found through bona fide instruction in one of Japan's cultural arts.) Sabi can be discovered while you sit alone in the peaceful silence of an old fishing town on an autumn nightfall or when you view a bright patch of green peeking through the snow in a mountain village.

A martial arts expert who throws his opponent with a single, almost imperceptible, effortless action is displaying sabi. (As opposed to achieving the same objective via numerous less efficient movements. The originator of judo, Kano Jigoro Sensei, expressed sabi through his principle of "maximum efficiency with minimum effort.") The same expert's humble, plain uniform, with a black belt worn all but white from age, declares a sort of beauty that cannot be detected in a Westernized gold lamé uniform and a new satin black belt. (Sometimes would-be American "experts," in an attempt to impress others with their depth of experience, will try to mimic this "worn" effect by scraping their belts with a wire brush. Unfortunately, this is simply silly, not sabi.) The natural beauty embodied by wabi and sabi can be seen in all Japanese arts, including calligraphy and painting.

Author Leonard Koren defines what he terms "the wabi-sabi universe" in the following way:[2]

Metaphysical Basis
- Things are either devolving toward, or evolving from nothingness

Spiritual Values
- Truth comes from the observation of nature
- "Greatness" exists in the inconspicuous and the overlooked details
- Beauty can be coaxed out of ugliness

State of Mind
- Acceptance of the inevitable
- Appreciation of the cosmic order

Moral Precepts
- Get rid of all that is unnecessary
- Focus on the intrinsic and ignore material hierarchy

Material Qualities
- The suggestion of natural process
- Irregular
- Intimate
- Unpretentious
- Earthy
- Murky
- Simple

SHIBUMI AND SHIBUI

Balanced imbalance, artlessness, solitariness, antiquity—all of this connects to wabi and sabi, which in turn have a connection with the terms "shibumi" (elegance) and "shibui" (elegant). "Shibumi" calls forth the image of something astringent in taste, while "shibui" suggests that which is unaffected or refined. In kado (flower arrangement, also known as *ikebana*), a shibumi flower arrangement evokes a feeling of coolness during a sizzling summer and warmth on a frosty day. That which is shibumi is quiet in refinement and soothing and satisfying to the heart in a manner that is not shaped exclusively by logic. It is the sentiment of "not too much," the use of aesthetic restraint in the finest sense.

Shibui indicates something that is not flashy (in color, for example), but ample in quality. Unpolished silver or gold and the color of ashes or bran can bring about a subdued yet elegant and serene shibui effect. The classical color scheme of a woman's kimono, a traditional martial artist's apparel of quilted *gi* (cotton uniform) and *hakama* (wide, skirtlike pants), the color layout of a Japanese guest room, the clothing and utensils in the tea ceremony—all evoke the attribute of shibui.

Zen has always placed emphasis on "Zen in daily life," or relating the meditative state to everyday activities. As a result, Zen monks have been expected to be able to display their enlightenment graphically through their brush writing.

Zen and Japanese Art

Zen is a school of Buddhism that was founded in the sixth century in India. Its founder is generally considered to be a monk named Bodhidharma (Daruma in Japanese). Shortly after founding Zen, he left for China around A.D. 520. There, according to oral tradition, Daruma sat facing a wall for nine years until he achieved enlightenment.

The term "Zen" comes from the Chinese word *Ch'an*, a derivation of the Sanskrit *Dhyana*. Zen was introduced into Japan from China by the monks Eisai (1141–1215) and Dogen (1200–1253). It was quickly embraced by Japan's military ruling class, and with its message of salvation through meditation it promptly made inroads into most aspects of Japanese life. Zen's emphasis on attainment of a state of oneness with the universe and being free from cerebral questioning influenced the entire Japanese cultural matrix, and many aesthetic qualities such as wabi, sabi, shibumi, and shibui can be said to have a historical correlation to Zen.

Due to its far-reaching historical influence in Japan, Zen has also affected most Japanese arts such as the tea ceremony, flower arrangement, and shodo. For some time in Japan, Zen priests (and the public as well) have believed that calligraphy can be thought of as a direct extension of the mind. Zen has always placed emphasis on "Zen in daily life," or relating the meditative state to everyday activities. As a result, Zen monks have been expected to be able to display their enlightenment graphically through their brush writing. Indeed, a number of them, such as Hakuin (1686–1769) of the Rinzai sect, were outstanding calligraphers/painters.

Zensho (Zen calligraphy) has been highly valued by the Japanese public despite the fact that while many Zen monks may be well trained in Zen, the depth of training has not always carried over into their artistic pursuits. (To put it bluntly, it is a mistake to think that all artwork produced by Zen priests is of a high caliber, even if it is confidently and spontaneously executed.)

Just like most other aspects of Japanese culture, Zen has naturally had an influence on Japanese brush writing, so there has been some borrowing of terminology. Zen first came into prominence in the West following World War II, when it was embraced by the beatnik generation. Along with this interest in Zen came an interest in Zen art, including calligraphy. As a result, Zen is intimately entangled with the history of shodo in America as well as in Japan. However, most schools of calligraphy do not identify themselves as Zensho, and while the calligraphy in *Brush Meditation* may be derived from a source of inspiration similar to the spirit of Zen, it is not Zensho. The same is true for the methods and techniques depicted in this book. Even though some over-lap of terminology and ideas may be present, this book does not deal with Zen Buddhism per se, although perhaps the material contained in these pages can be said to be imbued with Zen in a broad and generic sense.

Nonetheless, many schools of Zen make use of the ideas of ki and *hara*, which are also used in some schools of shodo.

Ki and Hara

While not exactly principles of art or design, the effective use of ki (life energy or spirit) and hara (abdominal centralization) can perhaps be considered part of the spiritual and technical aesthetics of all the Japanese arts. The terms have a long history in Japan, and they are a central component in traditional Japanese culture. Like so many aspects of the Japanese worldview, they are not always clearly defined, yet the ideas behind them are so much a part of the inherited Japanese consciousness that they have thoroughly permeated the language itself. For example, consider the word "ki." In an earlier publication of mine, *The Way of the Universe*, I wrote

> In Japanese, *byoki* means "sickness" and occurs when the spirit is weak. *Ki-chigai* is taken to mean "insanity," but it literally means "when Ki, or spirit, is wrong." *Ki ga kiku* directly means "when the spirit is sharply focused," but in everyday usage, it implies cleverness. *Ki ga chiisai*, or "when life energy grows small," is to be cowardly. *Jo Ki suru*, or "when the spirit is unsettled," is to be overly

34

excited. *Ki o ushinau* literally translates as, "when life energy is lost," and means to be unconscious. The Japanese have traditionally maintained the great importance of using one's Ki, or spirit, correctly, and they have indicated how Ki influences every aspect of life.[3]

"Ki" can be used to describe everything from a feeling to a natural phenomenon (such as weather) to the ki of the universe itself, or God. In a way, it can be regarded as the basic building block of nature.*

"Hara" means "abdomen," and it refers to a natural center in the lower abdomen that is used as a point of concentration in various meditative disciplines and Japanese arts. In Japan, the term "hara" holds a similar and equal importance to ki:

> If someone is brave, the Japanese say *hara no hito*, or "person of hara." A coward is *hara ga nai hito*—"a person with no hara." Understanding is indicated by *hara ga oki*—"a large hara," while a closed mind is *hara ga chiisai*, or "a small hara." A clear conscience is called *hara ga kirei*—"a clean hara," and someone with *hara ga kuroi*, "a black hara," is unfaithful. To become calm is *hara o suete*, or "to settle the hara."[4]

The mere fact that these words are frequently used in Japanese society should not be taken to indicate that all citizens of modern Japan

---

* Both ki and hara will be discussed at greater length in the following chapters; this section serves only as a brief introduction to two concepts that have a long history in Japan and that have influenced the evolution of shodo.

possess a deep or innate understanding of ki and hara. Consciously or unconsciously, it is for this very reason that many people in Japan seek out instructors of classical arts, such as Japanese calligraphy, that involve the development of these concepts. Even in Japan, however, it is relatively rare to find a teacher who can efficiently communicate these ideas, provide a concrete means of developing them, and then show how they can be utilized to enhance one's everyday life.

Shodo and Other Japanese Arts

Because all the Japanese arts share the same aesthetics, shodo enhances the study of budo, kado, and other art forms. The same feeling of balance that is needed for "sculpting" a successful flower arrangement is likewise needed in Japanese brush writing, in which every character must display a dynamic balance. In *odori* (dance) and the martial arts, participants should also master a dynamic or moving balance that is comparable to the asymmetrical balance used in Japanese calligraphy.

The identical unity with nature that is stressed in flower arrangement is also emphasized in the martial ways of aikido and *aiki-jujutsu*, while shodo demands an incredibly strict attention to detail and brush form that is not unlike the formal precision cultivated by pupils of ikebana. *Cha no yu* (tea ceremony) is based on *wa-kei-sei-jaku* (accordrespect-purity-solitude), and Japanese calligraphy and flower arrangement both seek to embody similar qualities. The tea ceremony's philosophical equation amounts to a particular expression of wabi, sabi, shibumi, and shibui. These artistic, perhaps even spiritual, characteristics are universal for all Japanese art.

Shodo and sumi-e allow you to comprehend these qualities in

SHIN-SHIN-TOITSU

Mind & Body
Coordination

Gyosho

such a way that their study can enhance the practice of different art forms. The opposite is true as well. Many Western students of various Japanese cultural arts frequently miss out on the importance of these ideas, and as a result have merely a pale copy of the genuine art that they are studying. This may be due to cultural differences, in some instances a language gap, and in other cases out-and-out ignorance. Nevertheless, studying one of Japan's cultural arts without a comprehension of these vital artistic principles is like trying to dine on the imitation food seen in front of Japanese restaurants. It may seem like the real thing, but it certainly doesn't taste like it, and the nutritional content is pretty meager.

The Universal in the Particular

Japan has traditionally excelled (due in part to the predominance of Zen) in spiritualizing comparatively ordinary activities such as brush writing, the preparation of tea, the military arts, and the arrangement of flowers. The goal is to perceive the whole of life through a particular enterprise or individual part of living. Master calligrapher, famed Zen adept, and founder of Muto-ryu swordsmanship Yamaoka Tesshu Sensei indicated that one of his main martial teachings was "the practice of unifying particulars and universals." He also wrote, in his *Notes on Kumitachi*: "Within these varied techniques there is deep meaning. Cast off subject and object, function as one; abandon self and others, form a single sword."[5] D. T. Suzuki, author of numerous books on Zen and Japanese art, likewise made reference to "the One in the Many and the Many in the One."

Consider a specific technique, or exercise to be copied, as a "particular." In shodo, for example, you do not copy a new character exclusively to learn to paint that symbol, and in sumi-e, you do not strive to make an accurate copy of bamboo or a bonfire solely to learn how to paint such individual pictures. Contained within a given lesson or particular technique is the essence of all techniques. You imitate and study a particular form to grasp the universal principles that allow the technique to work in the first place and that will finally enable you to transcend the form itself to discover the formless. In doing so, it is often possible to observe that these universal principles encompass something much greater than the individual art you are studying; they actually amount to vital lessons in living.

On an even more profound level, experts in flower arrangement speak of attaining a state in which they sense the inclinations and true characteristics of the flowers they will be arranging—a union with nature in which the particular (the artist) is united with the universal (nature). Martial artists, similarly, speak of a condition in which they become one with their opponent—or even multiple opponents—and eventually the universe itself. Perhaps then, the ultimate historical aesthetic running through all of the Japanese arts is a state of naturalness in which the distinction between individuals and nature dissolves into oneness.

Shodo and Personal Transformation in the West

Shodo's uniquely Japanese aesthetics and universal principles can not only serve to enhance the appreciation and understanding of other Japanese arts but can also have an impact on the way we engage in Western art. Shodo and other Japanese arts are steadily making inroads into Western culture precisely because of their universal aspects. Numerous Americans and Europeans are also drawn to shodo's universal spiritual message. For example, some Zen meditation experts, such as Omori Sogen Roshi and Terayama Katsujo Sensei, authors of *Zen and the Art of Calligraphy*, are enthusiastic supporters of shodo as a means of developing stronger powers of attention. Shodo is also valued as a method of cultivating the unification of mind and body in action. Several Zen educators have used shodo as a sort of "moving Zen."

Based on the number of teachers of other spiritual disciplines and Japanese arts found in shodo classes, it would seem that anyone would be able to utilize shodo as a mechanism for personal transformation, which could then be put to use in his or her specific art or calling. This has been one of the primary motivating factors for the gradual emergence of shodo in the West.

Contained within a given lesson or particular technique is the essence of all techniques. You imitate and study a particular form to grasp the universal principles that allow the technique to work in the first place and that will finally enable you to transcend the form itself to discover the formless.

Calligraphy teaches the artisan to realize a condition of comprehensive self-mastery. Western and Japanese practitioners of shodo cite expanded attention, improved peacefulness, stronger willpower, and deeper relaxation as just some of the advantages of their training. It is for this purpose that many devotees of shodo in Japan partake in calligraphy instruction in the first place. Classes are not taken exclusively to better your handwriting, as is regularly postulated; rather, Japanese students have come to actualize the personal gains that such a spiritual discipline has to offer and that, to many Westerners, make shodo so tantalizing.

SHODO AND ABSTRACT EXPRESSIONISM

As previously noted, Americans appear to have first come into contact with shodo and sumi-e following World War II. At that time, American artists were searching for something beyond the limitations of their own culture for motivation. Shodo inspired numerous abstract expressionist painters in the 1940s and 1950s, around the same time that avant-garde interest in Zen meditation was beginning to appear. Beat poetry was influenced by Zen and other forms of Buddhism, often as a reaction against materialism.

Abstract expressionist artists such as Franz Kline frequently chose to work in black and white, having been affected by monochromatic shodo and the minimalist aspects of Zen. In the 1990s, famed artists like Robert Motherwell, who has written of his lifelong interest in shodo, and Cleve Gray are executing works that are reminiscent of Japanese calligraphy. Motherwell, in fact, produced a series of paintings entitled *Shem the Pen Man* in homage to an expert calligrapher. These paintings feature a calligraphic ideograph suspended in a plot of color.

John Graham, author of *System and Dialects of Art*, has stressed the importance of spontaneous gesture and *écriture*, a French word meaning "calligraphy." He suggested that individualized écriture should evoke innovation in a calligraphic fashion that made use of "accidents." Graham, in turn, discovered and influenced Jackson Pollack, Willem de Kooning, Lee Krasner, and David Smith—four of the greatest abstract expressionists, who all produced works that are reminiscent of Japanese calligraphy. Al Reinhardt, after breaking away from cubism in the early 1940s, also turned to shodo for inspiration.

Art critic Barbara Rose has written about Japanese calligraphic art:

Since calligraphy neither depicts shapes nor closes contours, but maintains a fluid, fluctuating open form into which space may flow, it represents a system of marking ideally suited to an art style like Abstract Expressionism that sought to marry painting with drawing, eliminating the dichotomy between the two that exists in Western art, even in Cubism. The reconciliation of opposites, the unification of dualism is of course another Oriental concept especially attractive to Abstract Expressionists.[6]

Japanese artists and calligraphers noticed what was taking place in the American art world of the forties and fifties and were in turn influenced by the abstract expressionist movement. In 1951, noted artist Hasegawa Saburo wrote of Franz Kline's work and the fashion in which Asian art was altering abstract expressionism. This and other such articles began to affect Japanese calligraphers and painters.

In light of all this, it is evident that contemporary shodo is actually a spontaneous creative gesture that has as much in common with abstract expressionism as it does with the conventional written word. I make this point because I have found that many Americans have an interest in abstract art but are somewhat intimidated by the apparent "foreignness" of shodo. Once I explain the parallels and historical links between abstract expressionism and shodo, however, they are more easily able to relate to Japanese calligraphy.

SHODO AS A UNIVERSAL METHOD FOR REVEALING THE SPIRIT

After I explain to newcomers how shodo can function as a means of self-realization and meditation, many people express a sincere interest in learning more about this art form. I believe that this is because in shodo (unlike many other pursuits) one's degree of mental power becomes clearly and instantaneously seeable. Shodo makes the immaterial palpable in the form of smooth and elegant monochromatic designs. A person's authentic character is laid open through the brush, which, though less efficient than the pencil, is a most potent device for discovering the smallest wavering of mind or body. The pliant strands of hair in the *fude*, or brush, give birth to radiant, natural symbols that surpass divisions in nationality. Given, then, the universal character of this ancient Japanese way of the brush, and because of its pragmatic advantages, it is fairly clear why this art has landed on the shores of twentieth-century Europe and North America. Shodo and Japanese ink painting have a definite place in modern Western art and personal transformation.

HARA
Abdominal
Centralization
Gyosho

Chapter 2
MIND & BODY CONNECTION

PRIMARY PRINCIPLES FOR UNIFYING MIND, BODY, AND BRUSH

1. Use the mind in a positive way.

2. Use the mind with full concentration.

3. Use the body naturally.

*4. Train the body gradually, systematically,
and continuously.*

Standard shodo demands that the calligrapher brush every stroke perfectly; expert calligraphers and even beginners never go back to touch up any character or piece of artwork. Each movement of the brush must be performed with the full force of mind and body. There should be no faltering or indecisiveness.

In Japanese calligraphic art, as in living your life, you cannot go back, though in the beginning many novices lack the mental focus to paint the characters decisively. Every stroke must be delivered like the slice of a razor-sharp samurai sword, yet the brush must be handled in a serene manner. Gradually, the student's mental condition is altered

FIG. 8. A basic brush stroke, tapering to a fine point at the left.

through regular training. This transformation of consciousness can be carried over and applied to your daily life as well, even to academic and vocational pursuits.

Classical shodo demands (and develops) a complete union of mental and physical force. In spite of what most assume, it is surprisingly tough to make the mind and body work together as a unit. A seemingly uncomplicated feat, such as drawing a solid, straight line that tapers to a fine point, requires an unhesitating hand and mind. Figure 8 shows a

FIG. 9. The character *hito*.

basic brush stroke. Figure 9 shows the character *hito*, "human being." Notice how the left side of *hito* uses the tapering brush stroke seen in Figure 8.

Being capable of executing skillful brush strokes with genuine dexterity and decisiveness is an amazing challenge and can be attained only through the coordination of your mental and physical faculties. (If you'd like to try your hand now, skip to Chapter 4, where materials and basic brush strokes are introduced. After you've tried to reproduce the character *hito* just a few times, I think you will appreciate just how challenging it is to make the mind, body, and brush work together in harmony.) A powerfully focused mind commands the brush, and the brush is allowed to act as a perfect reflection of your mental movement. All fine arts, crafts, music, and a multitude of different activities call for this attitude of coordination. However, shodo ideally represents one of the greatest levels of harmony between thought and action: it both serves as a mechanism for depicting this unity and supplies a path for cultivating it. Both psychophysical coordination and the lack of it are unveiled on one's paper.

To arrive at a condition in which the mind precisely controls the body, and the body reflects this state, requires the growth of earnest concentration. It is this improvement of concentration that is needed for you to realize your full potential in shodo or daily existence. To fully realize how to arrive at such a state of attention and unification, it is necessary to examine the actual characteristics of the mind and body in detail.

Use the Mind in a Positive Way

The mind moves and regulates every part of the body, with the body ultimately reflecting our mental condition. Some of this regulation is being exerted unconsciously by means of the autonomic nervous system, through which the mind and body remain unified at all times. It is necessary to realize this if you are to competently learn any activity, including shodo, because the mind can positively or negatively sway the innate mind-body connection. (When this relationship is unstable, you may witness a Japanese character being painted by a teacher and comprehend it intellectually, yet fail to physically copy it on paper in the correct form.) This chapter explores the correct use of the mind, and later the body, as it relates to masterful mental and physical coordination in art.

Positive and energetic use of the mind is one of the most crucial points in learning Japanese painting and calligraphy, for without it we seldom have the determination to effectively master any other aspects of these arts. Beginners should consider the ways in which a negative attitude can influence the body. (Psychosomatic illnesses are but one example of the debilitating effect our mind can have on our body.)

Conversely, to be positive and decisive in art, as well as in life, is not the same as being inflexible or hard-headed. A truly positive mind has confidence in positive outcomes for most incidents, and is consequently capable of being at ease and adaptable in response to all circumstances. A positive mind has no reason to be upset or to resist, because it can confidently deal with every circumstance. It is this powerful state of mind that many shodo authorities have outlined as *fudoshin*, or "immovable mind," which again does not suggest rigidity but a confident condition of mental stability.

EXPERIMENTS WITH THE POSITIVE USE OF THE MIND

A positive outlook is most freely achieved through a conscious and rational examination of the nature of our thought patterns. Take a moment to reflect on the real, immediate state of your mind. Is your mental state positive? If it is not, what are the actual roots of this negativity?

We have all met people who see themselves as positive yet who are not seen by others in that way. The mind, being invisible, is easiest to view through an individual's expressions, actions, and posture. Japanese calligraphy, and indeed all forms of art, gives our bodies a means to make the invisible mind visible. For this same reason, psychologists will sometimes offer disturbed children crayons and paper to play with. By observing not only the drawings that are produced by these children but also the manner in which the sketches are created (confidently or hesitatingly, calmly or violently, and so on), the therapist can better understand the child's mental condition.

Hashimoto Tetsuichi Sensei, a top student of the late Nakamura Tempu Sensei, himself a leader in psychological development, wrote the following in his unpublished English interpretation of Nakamura Sensei's teachings:

> For example, if we say, "How hot it is today!" almost overwhelmed by the heat, then the attitude of our mind and our words are of a negative nature. But if we say, the degree of temperature is very high without being annoyed by the heat at all, then our attitude of mind and our words are not of a negative nature. This kind of differentiation we call self-examination or introspection, and on such introspection or self-examination, of course, we have to put our minds always in the state of positiveness, so that our words and deeds are also of a positive nature, making other persons feel at ease, happy and encouraged for the future.[7]

My Japanese yoga teacher, Hashimoto Sensei, has indicated that you must also consider the nature of your surroundings. Try putting this book down for a moment, and take a look around your house or apartment. Is it in order or disarray, immaculate or dingy? Your mind is affected by the words and behavior of others, by the appearance of your environment, and by a wide variety of elements. These elements amount to "suggestions" that we receive from our surroundings and circum-stances. Awareness of what is positive or negative or true or false in our environment, based on our understanding of the nature of reality (as opposed to how we were raised or our common cultural beliefs,

Shodo ideally represents one of the greatest levels of harmony between thought and action: it both serves as a mechanism for depicting this unity and supplies a path for cultivating it.

which may or may not be true), is vital for self-realization. Shodo, being a "way," has as its ultimate goal just such a state of self-realization. Again, shodo is not merely the act of manipulating a brush. Rather, the handling of the brush—as a specific and particular action—is primarily useful for helping us to discover broader truths that relate to every aspect of living. This book is an examination of these truths as they relate to daily life as well as shodo.

CREATING A POSITIVE ENVIRONMENT

By discovering the actual nature of our environment, we can attempt to restructure our surroundings so that our subconscious minds are affected in a positive manner. In Japan, a traditional calligra-pher's studio is usually neat and orderly. For the same reason, a classi-cal martial arts training hall is always tidy, uncluttered, bright, organized, and natural in look, as these factors alter the manner in which one learns. Before attempting the exercises and examples out-lined later in this book, take a moment to clean up the area where your painting will occur. Reflect on what the appearance of your room or home says about you.

By being conscious of the influences we receive from our surroundings, we can endeavor to be unaffected by the negative expressions, acts, and gestures of others, and in this way we can keep our minds free from pessimistic thoughts. For this reason, pupils of shodo or any Japanese art are discouraged from making negative remarks such as "I can't paint that character." Such a statement not only weakens them but has a dispiriting effect on others practicing in the same setting. You must always consider the effects of your words and behavior upon the other students in your class. (None of the Japanese cultural arts can be learned in great detail without a teacher, or in isolation, and discovering more positive and effective ways of relating to others is just one of the numerous benefits of studying these art forms.) Talking to people in a depressing fashion not only can weaken them, but can sadden them, which in turn taints your own surroundings. This vicious cycle is in fact a recurrent cause of lack of harmony within a school of art, a household, or even within civilization as a whole.

In the Japanese cultural arts, the cultivation of *wa* (harmony) is considered to be fundamental. Without this personal state of harmony, because the body and brush reflect the mind, one's calligraphy will become rough and unbalanced. Yet, we are not separate from others and our environment. This discovery means we need to consider the nature of harmony on both personal and interpersonal levels. Without harmony, a school of art (or even a nation) cannot operate effectively. But harmony can, at least to some extent, be developed by considering the effects of using positive, hopeful words when speaking.

THE POSITIVE ATTITUDE OF THE BUSHI

As you paint, and even in daily living, to keep the mind in the present is to unite the mind and body. The act of focusing your attention on the moment is not merely a component of shodo but is a feature found in all the Japanese arts, especially the martial arts and ways, where this idea has an exceptional and long tradition.

Budo (the martial way) is ultimately derived from the old traditions of the *bushi*, the classical warriors of ancient Japan. For a bushi (or samurai, as he was also known), facing the possibility of death was a common consideration. The bushi's mortality was regularly compared to that of the Japanese cherry blossom, which flowers just briefly, shows off lively hue and beauty, and is then scattered by the breeze. A bushi's principal responsibilities and code of morality focused on the notion of giving his life in the service of his clan and feudal lord. Relating to this part of *giri* (obligation) was the awareness that he could be required to lay down his life, without hesitation, at a moment's warning. To deal with the severity of this situation, some warriors resolved to live every day as if it were their last. They subsequently learned how to experience life thoroughly, without doubt or remorse. The bushi's aim was not to merely exist, but to live a rich life.

For the bushi to be capable of sustaining a positive attitude in the face of conceivable immediate death, he had to learn not to be troubled by either the past or, particularly, the future. This detail is also critical for the modern student of shodo and/or ink painting. Essentially, if the mind remains in the present, it is impossible to worry. We tend to worry solely about an occurrence that *has* happened or that *may* take place in the future. The immediate moment holds no time or space for worry.

One's past cannot be altered, and to become caught up in it is inefficient in terms of both time and effort. And by fearing for the future, we only drain ourselves, making us less capable of positively responding when the future is truly upon us. When worrying about a crisis that may or may not take place, we often end up experiencing the affair twice—once when imagining it and again when we actually undergo it.

Understanding the nature of keeping your mind in the present will make it possible to calmly face the paper you will paint on. (Because touching up is not allowed in shodo, fear is a very real possibility, especially when you are about to demonstrate the art in front of others.) When you rest effortlessly in the moment, no thoughts of past failures or future mishaps will be alive in your mind, and a genuinely positive mental state will come about. This is fudoshin, "immovable mind."

FOUR EXPERIMENTS TOWARD A POSITIVE MIND

To further your understanding of the power of a positive mind, try the following four experiments in your daily life. You may discover that they have a profound effect on how you function, and whether or not your mind and body are able to work as an effective unit. You may wish to work on just one of these experiments each day for four days.

1. Do you know what your mental state is from minute to minute? Why, and at what moment, does your state of mind change from positive to negative? This is an experiment in introspection or self-awareness.

2. What kinds of "suggestions" are you receiving from others and your environment? Are these influences positive or negative? Take note of each suggestion, remem-

bering that this is an experiment in the analysis of your surroundings.

3. From moment to moment, what is your attitude toward others? If it is not positive, observe yourself in relationship to others to discover where your negativity comes from and what effect it has on your environment.

4. Is your mind in the moment? When do you start to worry about the past or the future?

Self-examination under the above four circumstances can lead to a new, more positive way of using the mind. Taking note of the nature of negativity and seeing its source is an effective technique for unifying the body and mind and cultivating positive characteristics that are necessary for producing art. Never forget that it is the mind that moves the brush, and brush meditation reveals the character of the mind. When the mind is positive, the necessary unity of mind and body is preserved and you are able to display your full capacity. A negative mind will unconsciously retreat from the action presently taking place, which it consciously or subconsciously does not want to participate in. This causes a definite disconnection of mind and body, making one unfit to respond quickly to the ink's rapid interaction with the paper. In shodo, it is important to apply 100 percent of ourselves spiritually to what is taking place at the instant of painting. This positive mental condition is at times labeled *ki no dashikata* (the pouring forth of life energy).

KI AND THE POSITIVE USE OF THE MIND

We have all seen particularly positive and inspiring people, individuals who have a large presence. This invisible but tangible presence is ki, and it is a central part of shodo and Japanese art. (This same concept can be found in Japanese spiritual traditions and martial arts. For example, consider the martial disciplines of aikido and aiki-jujutsu. The expression *aiki* includes the symbol for ki, and it suggests an act of combining with the ki that pervades nature.) In *Japan: Strategy of the Unseen*, Michel Random defines ki as

> Energy. The manifestation of the vital inner energy that is to be found in every man, and which is none other than the original creative energy of the earth and the Universe. . . . Ki is thus the fundamental energy of being, beyond physical, chemical or natural phenomena. Attention, mental force is itself ki, and therefore it can be directed into every part of the body or turned outwards towards the external world.[8]

One of the easiest ways to release and focus your ki is by making use of positive visualization. In shodo, students can visualize ki flowing from their fingertips and through the brush as a means of connecting themselves spiritually with their brush. This results in a coordination of hand, brush, and mind, which in turn results in greater control of your brush movements. You can also think of drawing lines of ki on your paper, slightly preceding each brush movement, as a way of helping yourself to produce straight lines and balanced characters. The focused, concentrated use of the mind focuses your ki in a powerful manner.

All of the above methods of projecting and focusing ki help to facilitate the coordination of mind, body, and brush. They also have profound implications in daily life, which I hope you will experiment with and discover on your own. Many of these uses of visualization and ki, as well as simple means of actually testing the power of ki, will be explored later in this book. For now, try thinking of ki as a natural biological link between the mind and body. In this sense, your mind can be seen as a form of refined ki, while your body may be thought of as unrefined ki. In an even larger context, ki has been described as "the fundamental building block of the universe"—the one, indivisible element underlying all aspects of creation. The principal lesson to bear in mind is: ki amounts to the power that enlivens every living thing, and the positive operation of the mind liberates it while the negative use of the mind gives rise to *ki ga nukeru* (the withdrawal and the weakening of ki).

Use the Mind with Full Concentration

In shodo as well as the Japanese healing arts and martial arts, countless examples exist of phenomenal exploits and exhibitions of mental and physical expertise. These exhibitions are frequently thought to be examples of the force of ki. In many instances, however, these apparently superhuman capabilities can be attributed to the positive and concentrated strength of the mind applied in combination with the body's force. Therefore, it can be said that the effectiveness of one's ki, and the ability to make use of ki, is directly connected to an individual's aptitude for positive thought and close attention. Just as the assertive use of the mind unleashes the energetic force of ki, the focused use of the mind permits you to firmly influence and focus your ki. Like most other tendencies, attention is a state that must be cultivated. It is critical for shodo students to think about what sort of training will permit them to grasp the power of attention.

Quite a few activities, ranging from seated meditation to Japanese yoga (which I encourage my pupils to engage in), can be used to cultivate the strength of close attention. However, it is not only conceivable to attain exceptional concentration by engaging in everyday conduct, it is essential to do so.

EXPERIMENTING WITH THE POWER OF ATTENTION

When do you lose your concentration, and consequently give up your awareness of the moment? For most of us, it is when we are doing something habitual, such as putting on our socks. Try to recall which sock went on first this morning. Can you do it? As you learn to be aware of this type of break in attention, you will start to cultivate unclouded consciousness and pure attention in daily life as well as art. This exercise of unchanging awareness may lead you to a peerless state of mind that leaves no opportunities for slips of the brush.

Have you ever become so obsessed with the end result of an action that you failed to concentrate on the activity taking place at that moment? Take a moment to reflect on this. Many of us do it all the time. In shodo, some beginners are so concerned about eventually creating a great work of art that they do not adequately concentrate on the real learning process occurring at the present moment, and drift off into a

In the Japanese cultural arts, the cultivation of wa (harmony) is considered to be fundamental. Without this personal state of harmony, because the body and brush reflect the mind, one's calligraphy will become rough and unbalanced.

sort of fantasy world. When people are trying to finish an undertaking in haste, they are inclined to sacrifice concentration. This, however, does not mean that it is impractical to act promptly and still be able to pay attention. The point is that you should be certain that you are truly concentrating when in a rush.

Many folks also are disposed to turn off their concentration to do something that they assume to be boring. Beginning disciples of most Japanese arts (including shodo), for instance, grapple with the numerous repetitions of fundamental drills required by their teacher. They often grow bored, failing to recognize that the essence of these arts rests in their basics, which must be ceaselessly practiced if they are to become automatic responses. Their seniors generally have no difficulty training important brush strokes regularly, as they are steadily scrutinizing and refining detailed aspects of these proven fundamentals.

Whether or not you can pay attention is, at least to some extent, determined by whether or not you have a positive spirit. Even if nothing of appeal can be discovered in a particular activity, it is still possible to use that activity as an interesting experiment or practice to help your concentration. In fact, paying attention to those actions that you expect are of no worth is another technique for developing vigorous powers of attention. What you deem to be useless is, of course, relative. By actually paying attention to particular activities, you can often spot worth where you had imagined none was present. This is especially meaningful for beginners in shodo, who learn that this art is not based on short-term rewards, and that the genuine importance of many parts of practice becomes obvious only after quite a number of repetitions. Keep your mind centered on any bodily action or brush movement, even when it appears to be of slight benefit (understanding that no unconditional measure of value is likely). You may discover that this is an effec-tive means of cultivating potent attention.

People who decline to recognize the significance of concentrating will unwittingly cultivate the opposite tendency of not being able to pay attention even when they need to. Any repeated mental or physical act, whether positive or negative in character, starts to build up in the sub-conscious to form a habit. Plus, contemporary information in experi-mental psychology suggests that the more energetically and attentively we use our minds, the less worn out we become, on both mental and physical levels.

Bearing this in mind, it seems reasonable to adopt the samurai's principle of executing every feat in life as if it were for the last time. Using shodo and painting as a visible demonstration of your capability to unrelentingly utilize the mind in a positive and focused way, it is pos-sible to vitally transform yourself. It becomes natural to throw 100 per-cent of yourself into every moment, pour ki into each instant of life, become thoroughly alive, and truly live as opposed to only existing.

To further your understanding of the power of attention, try the following four experiments in your daily life. You may wish to work on just one of these experiments each day for four days:

1. How often do you fail to concentrate on that which you are familiar with? Try to notice the exact moment and activity that provokes this lapse in concentration.

2. Are you able to keep your mind on things you are try-ing to do in a hurry? Take note of when you become pre-occupied with the result of an action, and when you lose consciousness of the actual process you are engaging in.

3. How often do you disturb the flow of attention, and thus the flow of ki, by failing to concentrate on that which you think is not interesting? What happens if you actually pay attention fully during such an activity?

4. How often do you lose your awareness of the moment, and therefore your concentration, when you are forced to participate in something you feel is of little value?

People tend to lose their power of attention under the above four circumstances. Taking note of this tendency, seeing its origins, and being sure to focus the mind at these times is a supremely effective method for developing concentration. It is also an ideal way to unify the body and mind, invigorate your ki, and cultivate positive character traits that are absolutely vital for producing art. The above methods have a long tradition in Japanese yoga, and they are equally valuable to students of shodo.

Use the Body Naturally

We are born, exist, and die as an element of nature. This is fairly clear, but many men and women do not think about its real significance or how it connects directly to their lives. Merely being part of nature is no warranty that we will behave naturally. Plants or animals seldom conduct themselves in an unnatural fashion incompatible with their innate makeup. But human beings have free will and must make the decision not only to be part of nature, but to conscientiously heed the laws of nature. Being in harmony with nature vitalizes your ki, because ki amounts to the animating force of nature itself.

To relax and pursue your genuine makeup is to be in agreement with nature. Relaxation is indispensable for learning shodo, and while various instructors of the Japanese fine arts acknowledge this, they are frequently at a loss as to how they should communicate it. Without a relaxed state, it is hard to realize balance, beauty, and power in Japanese ink painting and brush writing.

Shodo must extend to other aspects of living beyond moving a brush on paper. (Otherwise you are simply engaging in *shuji*, or hand-writing, not "the way of sho.") Even if you can effortlessly create one masterpiece after another, this has slight significance if your body breaks down. When a shodo student experiences stress-related illness-es such as elevated blood pressure or persistent headaches, it is clear that he or she has failed to obtain all the different advantages that come from pursuing the art as a spiritual path. Ultimately, the idea of art in shodo is comprehensive enough to encompass the study of relaxation and calmness in action as a way of experiencing the art of living. While few individuals are required to paint every day, many of us experience daily stress, and shodo (when it is correctly practiced as a form of med-itation) can aid us in discovering the roots of nervousness and anxiety, as well as showing us how to resolve these problems.

If you do not discover how to stay cool during moments of pres-sure, it is doubtful that any of the methods you study will be fully real-ized. If you freeze mentally in a difficult predicament, you seize up bodily as well, and will be incapable of executing any competent action or brush stroke. Stressful moments arise as a matter of course in shodo and ink painting. The paper used for shodo can bleed easily if you pause too long. It can slip if too much pressure is applied to the brush, and because the brush hair is flexible you can never be absolutely certain which way it may twist or bend. To deal with uncertainty effectively and consistently produce art rather than pretty characters, you must understand the real nature of relaxation.

EXPERIMENTING WITH NATURALNESS AND RELAXATION

Try a simple experiment. Tense your arm as much as possible, and draw a circle rapidly in the air with your index finger. Do it over and over. Next, try relaxing your arm as much as possible, and draw the same rapid circle. For most of us, it is much easier to draw a quick, smooth, and dynamic circle in a state of relaxation.

Many people comprehend this, but few seem able to truly attain relaxation in activity. This is not because relaxation is unnatural or exceptionally complex. The dilemma stems from mistaken convictions and faulty habits (such as painting with the shoulders slightly lifted, which causes tense shoulders and headaches, instead of relaxing and allowing the shoulders to settle into their suitable spot naturally). Many either consciously or unconsciously believe that relaxation is comfortable but powerless. They think that relaxation does not permit a person to display noteworthy physical force. So, when they attempt to produce a particularly dynamic-looking character, they also frequently produce tension. This tension, in turn, creates something that, to the discerning eye, actually looks rough rather than dynamic. Some individuals have even come to believe that when they are relaxed they are not working seriously or giving their all.

Once this impression becomes part of your subconscious, it sways all of your conscious responses. In a pinch, or during a stressful moment while painting, you'll discover yourself unable to relax although you wish to. As you consciously teach yourself to relax and remain peaceful during troublesome moments in painting, you'll also cultivate the capacity to relax under pressure as a subconscious habit, which will influence your everyday life.

Understand that both positive and negative kinds of relaxation exist. For many of us, the difference between the two is not crystal clear. Clearing up the distinction between these two states has been spoken of in the Japanese fine arts, as well as martial arts, since antiquity. The *Tengu-geijutsu-ron*, composed in 1730, declares, "Weakness and softness are not the same. Rest and slackness again are not the same. Rest does not let go the living ki; slackness is near to dead ki."[9]

Positive relaxation suggests an energetic posture in which the mind and body are one. When the mind and body perform as a unit, we are in our most relaxed and serene condition, but we are likewise filled with energy. Negative relaxation is to relax without this structure of coordination. It is a form of physical and mental limpness, one that results in giving up vitality and alertness. Positive relaxation is filled with energy but does not contain unneeded tension.

In shodo, and in daily living, you want to grasp a posture and demeanor that is not tense or flaccid—an alive state that is poised between tension and limpness. Relaxation and collapse are not the same, and each causes opposite results in terms of mind-body oneness and the free flow of ki. As an experiment, try to notice in your daily life when you fall limp and when you grow tense. What is your state of mind at these times? When do you most often fall into these two conditions? By understanding the nature of tension—and its opposite, limpness—you can find the middle path of positive relaxation.

We often assume that the opposite of tension is relaxation, but is this true? By observing yourself in a state free from preconceived ideas,

66

you may discover that the opposite of tension is collapse, and relaxation is a different state altogether...a state balanced between and transcending opposites, in which your ki flows freely with that of nature.

THE HARA

One of nature's foundations is the law of gravity. This uncomplicated fact, like many others, has the capacity to bring about deep transformations in the way you choose to act in life and in calligraphy.

Because everything in nature tends to settle or drop downward, if you wish to relax and cooperate with nature, you need to permit the weight of your body to settle downward in a natural and relaxed manner. A stable and hence calm object's center of gravity has inherently settled to a comparatively low spot, while a wobbly object has a higher center of gravity.

Even if nothing of appeal can be discovered in a particular activity, it is still possible to use that activity as an interesting experiment or practice to help your concentration. In fact, paying attention to those actions that you expect are of no worth is another technique for developing vigorous powers of attention.

If you take up a thoroughly upright, aligned position that does not sag or cause you to slouch, your upper body's weight descends to a point beneath the navel. This place equates to your bodily center of gravity and center of balance. In the Japanese fine arts, healing arts, and martial arts, it is ordinarily alluded to as your hara, an idea with a lengthy and elaborate practice in Japan. According to Michel Random:

> The hara designates the area of the lower stomach, situated below the navel. For the Japanese this area is the

KOTOBUKI
Long Life,
Happiness
Sosho

original centre of man, the centre of psychic gravity where the deep vital forces are concentrated. It is through the hara that a man communicates with the primordial unity of all things.[10]

Traditionally in Japan, people have supposed that if a person is going to exhibit his or her highest power, he or she must center all strength in the abdomen. On one level, this widespread idea is accurate. More specifically, however, you must concentrate the mind's energy and attention in the lower abdomen, or *tanden*. Still more specifically, an individual should focus his or her energy at a point, or natural center, in the tanden. This point is frequently thought to be three *sun* beneath the bellybutton. ("Sun" is a traditional Japanese measurement; three sun is about 3.6 inches. The correct point for a larger-bodied Westerner may be even lower below the navel.) If you embrace an upright, relaxed posture, your center of gravity falls to this place in the lower abdomen, which conforms to your center of balance. By paying close attention to this point, you can securely coordinate the mind and body, obtaining a positive kind of relaxation. This accord of mind and body, in turn, results in an especially steady posture and vigorous psychophysical state. (It is crucial to remember that in shodo, if your posture is unstable, the characters you paint will also be wobbly and off balance. Yet, the means of arriving at stability of posture is not always what you assume it to be.)

This relaxed posture is amazingly powerful, and it is stable to the point of being outwardly immovable. (An example of the power inherent in a posture centered in the hara can be found on page 89.) In this condition you are immediately capable of rapid response and flowing brush movement. By regularly studying, via shodo, the distinctions between slackness, relaxation, and tension, you can impress these important differences upon the subconscious and in turn give birth to a vital or positive state of relaxation. In so doing, you can teach yourself to sustain a tranquil but vigorous condition in which you are equipped to confidently handle any emergency or stressful moment in painting.

By being mindful of your posture, you can cultivate a sort of usable relaxation, which, owing to its effective and vigorous constitution, can be put to use as well as preserved, even when you are under excessive pressure. Fundamentally, you need to sidestep a posture that is sagging and seems diminutive, collapsed, or withdrawn. You likewise want to avoid taking up a stiff posture when facing the paper to paint. Quick brush movement from such a position is troublesome. While you might be able to perform from a rigid posture given enough practice, and while an overly erect position has been advocated in certain shodo books, both are incompatible with free and spontaneous brush action.

When you use shodo to examine and expand your capacity to stay relaxed under strain, it becomes more than mere brush writing; it can be thought of as a moving meditation that permits you to cultivate genuine and unshakable composure. In shodo and in everyday life, serenity is strength.

Train the Body Gradually, Systematically, and Continuously

Shodo practice is a kind of physical activity, and it is necessary that training in this fine art be managed in a natural way. Without ease in training your body, you can rarely perform with maximum efficiency.

You can even sustain physical impairment, making ongoing practice difficult. Perhaps thinking of painting as a physical activity seems strange. But it is not uncommon for serious calligraphers to sit in one position for two or three hours at a time when giving lessons or working intently on a particular piece of art. If the body is held in a tense or unnatural way for an extended period of time, stiff shoulders and backaches are only two of the possible negative results. (Calligraphers and painters can fall prey to repetitive-stress-related problems such as tendinitis if the training of their body is not conducted in a natural, gradual, and regular manner.)

When poetry is painted on long sheets of paper, or if the artist is writing one large character using a big brush, the art of painting becomes even more physical in nature. Under such circumstances, we often squat over the paper, moving our bodies as we brush each stroke. In other cases, the calligrapher is standing but bending at a near ninety-degree angle and adjusting his or her bodily position as he or she paints. In shodo you paint with your whole body. If your artwork is produced on a small scale, your body movements are correspondingly small, but when you work on larger paintings, your physical actions grow in size. In Asia, it has traditionally been held that shodo and sumi-e experts enjoy exceptional health as well as longevity due to their cultivation of fine posture, calm and deep breathing, and physical flexibility.

In shodo, and in daily living, you want to grasp a posture and demeanor that is not tense or flaccid—an alive state that is poised between tension and limpness. Relaxation and collapse are not the same, and each causes opposite results in terms of mind-body oneness and the free flow of ki.

71

This state of improved health is only arrived at when you use your body naturally and train it continuously. Practicing irregularly does not produce results and allows the mind and body to fall out of condition. It is preferable to paint a modest amount on a continual basis than to practice a great deal from time to time.

Bear in mind that your body must be drilled in a gradual fashion to avoid future physical damage. How gradually an individual builds up to painting for longer periods is decided to a degree by that person's age and bodily state.

Your brain and body are in a perpetual state of change. The remarkable benefits of shodo training rest in a lifelong process of participation. If you discontinue your practice, no matter how long you have been painting or how skillful you are, both your soundness and competence will decline. Shodo training is helpful only as long as one is, in some manner, truly engaging in it.

Once in a while, students of the Japanese cultural arts question if the liberal amount of time they put into their training is worth what they are getting out of it. While this appears to be a sensible inquiry, it actually reveals a basic lack of comprehension about the Japanese arts, which is, sadly, not unusual. In essence, the time you put into the training of an art *is* what you are getting out of it. The process of practicing is what's actually helpful, not some future aim or outgrowth of practice. All of existence exists exclusively at this moment. The past and the future, in a way, dwell only in our thinking as self-constructed, artificial realities. In the classical Japanese arts, you must train to repose calmly in the instant, and in your timeless perception of the moment, you grasp a state transcending duality—a condition that is both everlasting and boundless.

Shodo training is the objective. Accordingly, to practice shodo with authentic awareness is also to realize the superior benefits of shodo itself.

Through gradual, uninterrupted, and systematic shodo exercise, you can continue developing even as you grow old, because the art is essentially a never-ending meditation. Shodo is an art form that has existed for generations in Asia and still remains capable of vitally improving the lives of its followers for many generations to come.

KEI
Respect
Sosho

Chapter 3

UNITING MIND, BODY & BRUSH

1. Grip the brush gently and focus your ki through the brush tip.

2. Before touching the paper, the tip of the brush must be calm.

3. Relax to let the brush move naturally and with rhythm.

4. The brush follows the movement of ki.

5. Do not cut off your stream of attention.

Obviously, the brush does not move by itself. Remember, it is the mind that moves the brush (or *fude* in Japanese), and any legitimate study of technique must be accompanied by a parallel investigation into your psychological state. Your brush is a kind of surrogate for your own degree of spiritual development. That is the fundamental premise of this book, and to the extent that you master the principles for brush control and meditation that follow, you are in a better position to broaden yourself spiritually. You will also have a far better chance of producing top-notch calligraphy.

Grip the Brush Gently and Focus Your Ki through the Brush Tip

Physically speaking, shodo begins with the student's grip on the brush. Unless a suitable technique of gripping is mastered, no advancement is possible. Figure 10 and Figure 11 show the correct method of holding the brush. Examine the photos closely, as several important points are illustrated.

First, your elbow should not stick up or out to an excessive degree. This would only create an unsettling of the arm's weight as well as produce tension in the muscles of the arm and shoulder. This tension can cause your flow of ki to clog in the shoulders and not be effectively transmitted through the brush into the painting. This point is important, and various Japanese calligraphy authorities have made note of its significance. In *Zen and the Art of Calligraphy*, the Zen master Omori Sogen Roshi, referring to his calligraphy teacher, writes:

> The work of a Zen artist, on the other hand, is permeated by what Hakuin called the "overwhelming force of enlightened vision." That force is *kiai*. Ki, the energy of the cosmos, is always present but remains dormant if not cultivated. Kiai is to be full of ki; it is incorporated in the ink as *bokki*.
>
> Setsudo wrote that "bokki is not, as most people believe, the colour of the ink, and does not depend on the quality of the brush, ink, and paper. If one's ki is not extended into the work, the bokki is dead." The clarity of the bokki is not seen with the eyes, it is sensed with the

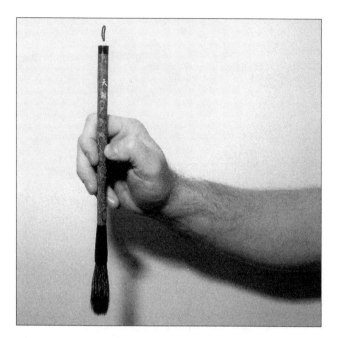

FIG. 10. Hold the brush stem perpendicular to the paper and bend the wrist slightly backward. The grip is supple but firm.

hara, the physical and spiritual centre of one's body. Bok-ki reveals the calligrapher's inner light.[11]

At the same time, do not let your elbow sag or droop. As discussed on pages 65–67, positive relaxation is not the same as a state of collapse. When your elbow sags heavily toward the ground, it also tends to rub against the body and produces a cramped feeling that is expressed in your artwork. You should feel that your elbow is floating in a settled position a few inches from your body.

Next, notice that the brush stem is perpendicular to the paper. This can only be accomplished if your wrist is allowed to bend somewhat backward. If the top of your wrist bends upward, so that your palm turns in toward you, your elbow will also come out and your arm's weight will grow unsettled. Tension is created yet again.

FIG. 11. Do not let your elbow stick out or droop but hold it in a state of "positive relaxation."

Some instructors have tried to abruptly pluck the brush from the student's hand as a means of testing the handhold.[12] An ink-covered hand would announce an incorrectly controlled fude. Squeezing tightly is not the solution, because this does not generate graceful, dynamic characters. Flaccidly gripping, on the other hand, results solely in a loss of brush control. It is imperative to find out how to grasp the brush in a manner that is neither tight nor slack, with a sort of "alive" handhold in which your ki is propelled from downward-pointing fingers through the fude, out of the tip, and into the paper. This supple but firm hold is vital and has been characterized as *ki de toru* (grasping with ki).

Following are four experiments that will help you learn not only how to hold the brush correctly, but also how to harmonize your mind and fude.

EXPERIMENT #1

Grip the center of the brush stem as illustrated in Figures 10 and 11. Ask a friend to grasp the top of the brush stem. Focus your mind on the place on the brush that your friend is holding. At this point, he or she, while holding the brush stem from above your grip, should start to slowly and gently lift upward. Note how much force is required to make the fude slip from your fingers or to cause your entire arm to come up (if your grip is not lost).

Now, holding the brush firmly but without tension, visualize a stream of ki flowing through the brush stem, through the bristles, into the paper, and continuing endlessly. The other person should try to gradually pull the brush stem upward again, slowly so as not to cause a loss of concentration, and using the same force as before. If your concentration and stream of ki are unbroken, the fude should be much more difficult to move, if it is not, in fact, immovable. (In this way, you become one with the brush, it will easily follow your mental commands, and accurate painting is much more readily accomplished.) This is an experiment, not a sort of competition, so it involves calmly comparing two different states, utilizing similar amounts of force.

EXPERIMENT #2

Next, try concentrating on the area of the brush stem that you are grasping, thus stopping the movement of ki in that spot. Your partner applies upward pressure as before. The brush will probably move. Follow that action by focusing ki through the brush, out of the tip, and continuing infinitely. This time, the brush grip should remain undisturbed. In each case, your friend should gradually pull up on the brush stem. Make sure that you do not shift your point of attention when pressure is applied to the brush.

If concentration is maintained, and you do not tense up when your friend pulls on the brush, the grip on the fude will be extremely solid. This reveals a central point in shodo: if the mind becomes attached to a particular thought or place, and the movement of ki freezes, mind and brush coordination and control is lost. Kobara Ranseki Sensei emphasizes that your mind should not be stuck on the brush but should instead be directed toward the brush strokes taking place on your paper. In a special article written for the *Nihon Keizai* newspaper, Kobara Sensei elucidated:

> I always explain when [my students] eat delicious food, at that moment, they become unconscious of the eating utensils. Shodo is just the same as this. They must be unconscious of, and transcend the brush, thus acting spontaneously. To accomplish this, students must practice severely, every day, until they forget the brush, and make strokes freely. Calligraphers should not worry about gaining the teacher's admiration, or putting their art in exhibitions. They must forget the brush, and simply practice in a state free from anxiety about results.[13]

EXPERIMENT #3

This experiment involves a more physical perspective with the flow of ki. Take a look at Figure 10 and Figure 11 again, and notice that the fingers gripping the brush are pointing downward, roughly perpendicular to the paper and in line with the movement of ki. This grip unifies the mind and brush.

Hold the brush incorrectly, so that the fingertips point toward a wall (parallel to the paper), but focus your mind on the tip of the brush as before. Ask your friend to pull up as before. Most likely, the brush will be moved despite your downward focus of attention. This clearly shows that not only must ki be directed toward the paper, but your fingertips must also be pointed in a similar direction. The mind and body must function as one.

Now, imitating the photo (with your fingertips pointing downward) and directing ki from the brush tip, ask your friend to pull up on the fude. If you are gripping correctly, the brush will be glued to your hand. (Another central point when holding a fude is to make sure that you grip with your fingertips, not your fingers or the sides of your fingers. This is not to say that the sides of the fingers and knuckles are not in contact with the brush stem, but that the main points of contact are the fingertips.)

Before Touching the Paper, the Tip of the Brush Must Be Calm

With practice, unifying your ki with the brush and holding the brush correctly become unconscious actions. For beginners, however, briefly checking your grip and aligning your ki with the brush is a necessary first action. Next, note if the tip of the fude is motionless or shaking. A swaying brush not only makes it hard to paint stable characters, it reveals a rickety, nervous mental condition. Again, in shodo the body reflects the mind. When your brush tip starts to tremble, this is often an indication of a break in composure and concentration and is an opportunity to lose control of the brush. By studying shodo, it becomes clear that in art, as in daily life, the mind and body are interconnected.

Suppose you notice that the tip of your fude is wobbling. One common reaction is to squeeze the brush more tightly, or in some way try to restrain its movement. Unfortunately, this usually only causes the brush tip to shake even more. Why? Imagine you are sitting in a pool of water. You notice that the water is not calm; you are surrounded by waves. One reaction is to take your hands and rub them across the surface of the water in an attempt to smooth out the waves. Obviously, trying to force the water to be calm will only make more waves. If you simply sit still, assuming no other external forces are at work, the waves will gradually diminish of their own accord. All water contains waves, but the closer you come to doing nothing, the more the size of the waves reduces.

If the mind becomes attached to a particular thought or place, and the movement of ki freezes, mind and brush coordination and control is lost.

Likewise, we all give off a brain-wave pattern, but some patterns are more calm than others. Your brush tip is a reflection of your brain waves, and the more you try to force it to be still, the more "waves" you create in your mind. (In a related example, many of us have figured out that if we deliberately try to fall asleep, our very desire to sleep will frequently keep us awake.)

Sometimes, even though you feel like you are doing nothing, your brush tip and mind continue to shake. In such a case, to paraphrase Zen, you can try doing something that leads to doing nothing. Following is an exercise in calmness to help you understand this more fully.

EXPERIMENT #4

Hold the brush correctly above the paper. With your elbow down and in the proper position, move the brush repeatedly from left to right in an arc of about a foot. As you do this, focus your mind intently on the movement of the brush tip. Gradually make the size of the arc smaller and smaller. Keep your mind centered on the brush tip, and your brain-wave pattern will also grow smaller as well as calmer. In a short while, the movement will become so small that it is not outwardly discernible, but be sure to let the feeling of stillness that has just been generated continue infinitely.

If you are having trouble imagining what all of this should look like, tie a rock or relatively heavy object to a string. Start it swinging from side to side, then do nothing but hold your hand still. The object's arc will gradually become smaller and smaller, until it seems to be hanging motionless. You are doing something similar with your brush, except that you want to allow the sensation of endless reduction to continue within you. Once you get the hang of it, this trick should help you to calm the movement of your fude even when your projection of life energy through the brush has not been sufficient. This exercise is not only an effective means of stilling the brush and mind, but has the ultimate potential to lead you to a state of transcendence that is both endless and eternal.

Relax to Let the Brush Move Naturally and with Rhythm

Shodo has a visible rhythm. Although the kanji (Chinese characters) are at rest on the paper, they must seem as though they are in motion. This is *dochu no sei* (stillness in motion), which is frequently alluded to in esoteric manuals of Japanese philosophy and religion. Its opposite is "motion in stillness." The harmony of these two conditions results in accomplished shodo.

Shodo is moving meditation, and as such it acknowledges that we are repeatedly in motion in daily activities. You must learn to remain calm and relaxed within action if you wish to translate the meditative state into your life. Shodo will help you discover exceptional levels of calmness in the midst of dynamic activity.

Before performing any action, including brush movements, it is important to center yourself in the lower abdomen. With a fully erect posture, relaxed but not limp, your upper body weight will reach its highest point of density in the hara. Concentrating on this spot is a helpful way to facilitate the settling and stabilizing of your body's weight and has a calming effect on the mind.

As you move the brush, you must maintain a posture that is relaxed, upright, and aligned. Figure 12 illustrates the correct posture for sitting in a chair. Figure 13 shows the proper position for sitting in *seiza*. (Seiza is a traditional Japanese way of sitting that is used for both meditation and painting. You sit lightly on the heels, with the big toes crossed on top of each other and some space between the knees. Although seiza is difficult at first, it is particularly effective for centering your weight forward and down into the lower abdomen. When you're

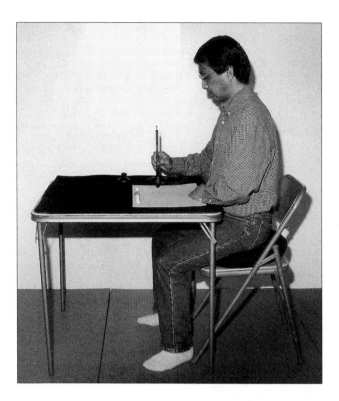

FIG. 12. The correct posture for sitting in a chair. Keep your feet flat on the floor or tucked under the chair so that you maintain a natural lumbar curve and shift the weight toward the front surface of the lower abdomen.

painting large pictures or calligraphic works, it is often advisable to stand. However, none of the painting exercises depicted in this book require standing.)

Several points are important if you are to take up a correct posture and paint freely. Do not slump or raise the shoulders, as illustrated in Figure 14. Sit down lightly, almost as if your bottom were sore, and maintain a posture that looks big, as discussed on page 67. Make sure that your table is not too high, as this can cause your shoulders to rise and tension to form.

Often when you're painting, you'll find that your head starts to sag forward while your neck collapses, bends, shortens, and produces a hump at its base. The rest of the spine soon curves in on itself as well.

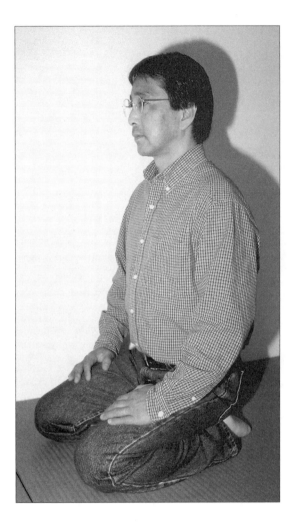

FIG. 13. The correct position for sitting in seiza. Seiza is effective for centering your weight forward and down into the lower abdomen.

You can alter this by centering yourself in the hara and by correcting your posture with the movement of your head. Mentally release your muscles, particularly along the neck and spine. Visualizing your hara as a sort of anchor, direct the top of your head up and away from your hara, then draw your chin and head back into alignment with your lower abdomen. Allow your spine and neck to lengthen until your posture is aligned. (Envisioning the muscles along the spine growing longer

86

FIG. 14. This spine and shoulder posture is INCORRECT. Letting your head sag forward brings the neck and back out of proper alignment. To correct this, recenter the hara and adjust your posture by repositioning your head.

and wider is an effective technique to use at this point.) If you concen-trate deeply and relax, your body will move slowly into the correct posi-tion with little conscious effort on your part. But be careful not to force your body into an overly erect posture.

By relaxing and using visualization, you should also let your chest expand while your back and shoulders widen. In most cases, your ears, shoulders, and pelvis should be parallel to the floor, as is your table and paper. Your head, shoulders, and pelvis should not be twisted. Avoid sitting with legs outstretched, as this causes your pelvis to roll back-ward and your lumbar region to curve outward in a slump. When you're sitting in a chair, try to keep your feet flat on the floor or tucked under the chair (almost as your legs tuck under your hips in seiza). This maintains your natural lumbar curve, and it shifts your weight toward the front surface of the lower abdomen—exactly where you want to center your weight and mind in the hara. Relax your face and eyes, and find the most comfortable posture within the context of the above instructions.

Because this act of centering produces a particularly steady position, it frees you to move your hand and brush in an open, easy manner. To sustain this free and relaxed condition of stability, avoid leaning in an unbalanced way, as the upper body's weight must be in equilibrium at the hara.

All of the above postural points can be practiced in daily life and should result in a healthier, more tension-free life.

EXPERIMENT #5

This experiment will give you some idea of the power and stability of sitting with hara. In *Meditation Gut Enlightenment: The Way of Hara*, Haruo Yamaoka describes a means of testing the unique power of this natural center in the lower abdomen:

> Sit seiza (legs underneath). Fill your mind with thoughts and tense the muscles in your shoulders and neck. Next, have someone stand behind you, place his hands on both sides of your hip area, and push. He will be able to slide you across the floor very easily. If he should push around your shoulder area, you will fall over.
>
> Next, while you are in the same position, remove all tension from your shoulders and neck. Relax your arms.

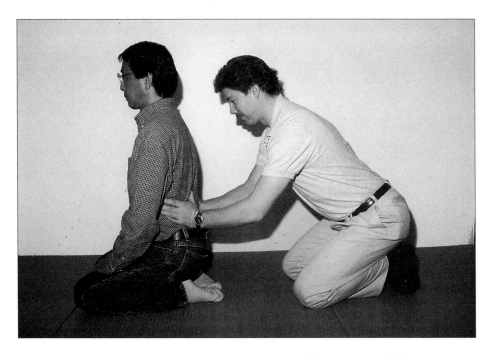

FIG. 15. Ask a partner to help you test your ability to stabilize the mind in the hara and realize a deeper sense of body-mind coordination.

In other words, relax the upper portion of your body. Focus on your hara. As you focus on your hara, your mind will become empty naturally. Ask your partner to push from behind as before. This time he will not be able to slide you across the floor. You will be firm, rigid, but relaxed. Most important, you will be in balance.[14]

Figure 15 shows what is being described here. Slowly and carefully try this experiment, as a means of grasping correct posture, learning more about stabilizing the mind in the hara, and understanding the power derived from doing so. (Remember, in life and shodo the body

POEM BY RIKYU
*Sosho kanji,
hentaigana, kana*

*In your practice
Start by learning one
And continue until you understand ten.
From ten you must return
To the original one.*

Keiko to wa
Ichi yori narai
Ju o shiri
Ju yori kaeru
Moto no sono ichi

mirrors the mind.) This is not only an experiment but a challenge to your ability to remain composed under pressure. You may have to practice for a while to achieve these results. Nonetheless, by performing these exercises with a partner in a gentle, noncompetitive style and freeing the mind from anxiety about results, you can realize a deeper sense of body-mind coordination.

In addition to being centered and focusing the mind at your hara, you also need to hit upon a kind of relaxed concentration. In *The Anatomy of Change*, Richard Heckler advises:

> It is important to remember that center is a state of being that is not confined to a certain posture or a constantly held image. . . . It is not that we have to find our center and then maintain it at all costs. Center is more a reference point to return to, so we can relate to our life situations in a complete way. . . . Sweeping through our bodily dimensions with the attention, to feel an overall balance, is the first step in touching the state of center. We line up our structure in order to touch that balance within. Being in balanced form opens the opportunity to feel oneself, and the dimension of feeling is directly related to center.[15]

Once you are centered in the hara, the body relaxes, and if that centering continues, the body remains relaxed. This is essential to avoid impeding the flow of ki, and in turn the dynamic flow of the brush itself. If you are to practice shodo as moving meditation, relaxation is vital. Relaxation, however, comes only with naturalness. If you feel tension in any part of your body during any brush movement, it is necessary to examine your posture and way of moving for unnaturalness. (The brush movement might be overextended or cramped by poor posture.)

THE FEEL AND RHYTHM OF RELAXATION

How can you tell, with any certainty, that a position or action is truly relaxed and natural? Try pausing at varying points in the painting process. Hold the position for thirty seconds or so, and notice if you can feel the muscles in any part of your body. If you detect a strong muscular sensation in any body part, what you are sensing is usually tension.

Muscles that are fully relaxed produce no powerful sensation, so you should be able to freeze at any time and in any position while painting and not feel your muscles. (If you cannot, you are moving in an unnatural manner, and it is vital to realize what kind of motion or posture is producing the tension and alter it.) When you create no sensation of tension, you are painting correctly. You become unconscious of your body and self. This, of course, is not numbness or a lack of awareness; it is a serene condition, so relaxed as not to be felt. At any moment of peak performance, in any activity, people tend to forget themselves. They are aware only of the instant and the action taking place. This is *muga-ichi nen*, (no self–one thought), and it is this mental state that allows shodo to transcend mere skillful writing.

You must learn to remain calm and relaxed within action if you wish to translate the meditative state into your life. Shodo will help you discover exceptional levels of calmness in the midst of dynamic activity.

KIYO
Pure, Innocent
Sosho

As you continue to move the brush, maintain a constant cadence. Rhythm both indicates and promotes coordination, and all arts, including shodo and ink painting, have a unique rhythm. Each Japanese character has a particular cadence with which it is painted. Find the correct rhythm and maintain it to excel in painting. Breaks in rhythm reveal breaks in coordination of your body and mind. They usually happen when the flow of ki is broken during a lapse in mindfulness or a moment of tension.

The stream of life energy must continue in a stable rhythm from one character to the next until a line of words is completed. Your entire composition ought to sustain a unified appearance of rhythm. (Beginners should remember that lines of Japanese characters are traditionally written from right to left on a page, and in shodo characters are usually painted from the top of the paper to the bottom.) To produce this dynamic yet balanced feeling, the brush flows in an unconstrained and easy form within each character. Every kanji and kana has a predetermined number of strokes that must be brushed in a strictly defined order.

STROKE ORDERS FOR RHYTHMIC SHODO

While it is always possible to look up a kanji's correct stroke order in a Japanese-English kanji dictionary, the following simple rules are helpful for beginners trying to master rhythm in shodo:

1. The brush stroke order is from top to bottom of a kanji.

2. The brush stroke order is from left to right of a kanji.

3. When two or more brush strokes cross, horizontal strokes precede perpendicular ones (but there are some notable exceptions to this rule).

4. Paint the center component of a kanji first, then the left, followed by the right components.

5. If a perpendicular line runs through the center of the character, it is painted last.

6. Right-to-left diagonal brush strokes precede left-to-right diagonal strokes within a kanji.

These points should help in getting acquainted with the stroke order of Japanese phonetic symbols and Chinese characters, which is essential for a consistent rhythm. (Perhaps the most basic rule is to check a dictionary when in doubt.) Remember that within the framework of each character, the brush should move smoothly from one stroke to the next.

Once you start to practice the various compositions in this book, you will have a chance to work with rhythm in shodo. To help facilitate an unbroken rhythm and flow of ki, try counting out loud as you make each brush stroke. (In many cases throughout this book, you will find small numbers next to each brush stroke in a given kanji. These numbers indicate stroke order but can also be used to help master rhythm.) Try to count each stroke as you would a musical beat. Allow about one second per beat.

As you progress in shodo, you will discover that the rhythm between (and during) certain strokes will speed up but at other times

WA
Harmony
Sosho

will slow down. This is something that must be learned with a qualified teacher and through ongoing experience. While the rhythm of the strokes is rarely broken in shodo, you will not necessarily always paint at the same speed at varying points within a character. This is particularly true as you become more advanced in the art.

In a larger context, nature has its own rhythm. To discover that rhythm, through shodo and/or painting, is a fascinating and never-ending pursuit. Your highest objective in shodo, then, is to become one with the vibrant rhythm of nature and to let this pulsation flow out through the brush.

The Brush Follows the Movement of Ki

Your spirit controls your brush or, in everyday life, your body. For a split second, the student needs to powerfully concentrate on the character to be painted, and then without faltering move the brush in a relaxed fashion. In this way, the artist prevails mentally before even contacting the paper.

Practice seeing the image on paper before you move the brush. The instant you have a clear picture in your mind, apply the brush to the paper without the slightest delay. (While the mind moves first, it does not separate from the body but dynamically leads the brush into action.) The trick is to paint the character with your ki first, that is, mentally, and move the brush with the positive sensation of having already succeeded.

Central to this technique is developing sufficient concentration to first produce a clear mental image and then, decisively and with absolutely no hesitation, move the fude. In time, this becomes automatic, and an image is created in one second while the brush moves in the following second. A similar mental process can be used in most daily activities to harmonize the mind and body and, consequently, achieve greater results with less strain.

If you are a novice, try drawing the shape in the air over the paper two times while focusing the mind deeply on the action taking place. On the third repetition, paint the image. This is a more lengthy version of the same concept.

When ki dynamically leads the fude into action, a unity of mind, body, and brush is attained. This state of unity is both profound and all-encompassing, as writer Michel Random explains:

> Internal awareness, real efficiency, the accomplishment of every action, all require the union of body and mind. The energy which effects this union is called ki. It obeys the mind which can direct it, cause it to concentrate on one area, and make it flow.
>
> The meaning behind these words lies in a single fact, for ki, the fundamental energy of the universe (which connects and relates all things), is also the true body of things in the subtle sense. From there on, it can combine with breath and spirit and, in turn be the very emanation of breath and spirit.
>
> Ki is life itself. As long as ki exists, life continues. When the vital energy disappears, life ceases. The control of ki, therefore, represents control over life, health, harmony, and therefore energy.
>
> If ki gives at least a spiritual immortality, this is

because ki is the energy or original force which has been present ever since the creation of the universe and because this force is independent of time and space.

This concept explains why, as man is the emanation of universal nature, all consciousness stems from and returns to nature which is a common book for all of mankind.[16]

Do Not Cut Off Your Stream of Attention

Unless you preserve an uninterrupted flow of attention, the rhythm that gives your characters a dynamic demeanor will be shattered. Many people tend to cut off their stream of concentration at the culmination of an action. In calligraphy, this regularly takes place when an individual character or a line of words is completed. But in shodo, you must retain an uninterrupted flow of ki and close attention throughout the creative action.

This mental follow-through leads to an undisturbed state of peaceful awareness. Skilled painters' brush movements will often continue through the air, sometimes for a few inches, after the brush leaves the paper. In particular, when you're painting a stroke that tapers to a point at the end, you should not stop the brush abruptly after completing the action. Let the movement of ki continue by following through with the motion of the hand and mind as the brush is lifted from the paper. This is similar to the follow-through used in a skillful golf swing, or the batting of a talented baseball player.

The movement of ki continues even when contact with the paper is broken. This correlates not only to an act of mental and physical fol-

99

low-through, but also to sustaining a flow from one character to the next. Although various characters are not visually linked by brush lines, they should always project a feeling of connection. This is known as *ki-myaku* (the unbroken pulse of ki).

In a broader sense, if you are to practice art as meditation, you need to retain your awareness of the present from the time you pick up your brush until the moment you cleanse it of ink. In the beginning, you may only maintain this heightened state of concentration for a few minutes. With practice, you'll realize that keeping attention rooted in the moment not only results in integration of mind and body but also amounts to entering into a condition beyond time. Because the act of trying is predicated upon your desire for some future result, it actually interferes with recognition of what is taking place in the instant. Perhaps the secret lies in uniting the mind and body and simply painting with a watchful attitude—an effortless state in which action occurs naturally. During pure observation of the instant, you may see what actually *is*, not what was or what you hope will be in the future, but the genuine nature of existence. If this observation is motivated by fear or the hope of reward, it is no longer pure.

At any moment of peak performance, in any activity, people tend to forget themselves. They are aware only of the instant and the action taking place. This is muga-ichi nen (no self—one thought), and it is this mental state that allows shodo to transcend mere skillful writing.

Learn to cultivate a condition of watchfulness without motive. In such a condition, you have an opportunity to see all things as they truly are, including your own thoughts. Is there, then, a separation between the mind that thinks and that which is thought of? Between the artist observing the process of creation and that which is observed? Between the artist who experiences and the experience itself?

It is my contention that, ultimately, no such distinctions exist. Reading about all of this has little value. Actually investigating pure attention, which contains no remnants of time but instead only what *is* —the absolute and eternal unity of all creations—this has tremendous significance.

FUDOSHIN
Immovable
Mind
Gyosho

Chapter 4

LESSONS IN BRUSH MEDITATION

While some books cover shodo techniques in detail, few books deal with the manner in which Japanese fine arts function as forms of spiritual realization. Because the meditative and aesthetic sides of shodo and ink painting are the main focus of this book, no attempt has been made to present an extensive series of technical lessons. Instead, this chapter offers a short series of exercises and compositions of varying degrees of complexity for you to experiment with. Although this chapter delves into the art of the Japanese brush, what is offered here will only be meaningful when studied as a visible expression of the principles of self-mastery that have been presented thus far. If you find it difficult to reproduce the compositions here, review the previous chapters with an eye toward more successfully integrating the meditative principles outlined with the technical material in this section.

If you want to begin serious study of any Japanese fine art, you need a competent teacher. Following this chapter is information about how to find an instructor and painting supplies.

Setting Up

Preparing to paint is neither time consuming nor expensive. You will need the following items to copy the compositions presented in this chapter:

a medium-sized brush *(chu-fude)*
a small brush *(ko-fude)*
an ink stick *(sumi)* or liquid ink *(bokuju)*
an ink stone *(suzuri)*
paper *(kami)*
a paperweight *(bun-chin)*

These are shown in Figure 16.

BRUSH

There is no standard regarding what constitutes a large, medium, or small brush in shodo. The medium-sized brush I recommend in this book has bristles about two inches in length, while the small brush's bristles are a little under one inch long. In general, buy the highest-quality brush you can afford. A bad brush only makes shodo more difficult for a novice.

INK STONE

Many different kinds of ink stones are also available. These can range in price from ten dollars to ten thousand dollars. The variable factor affecting the cost of the stone is the type of stone and its quality. Carving also has some impact on price, but not performance. Buy the most expensive stone you can find and/or afford. Try to get a natural,

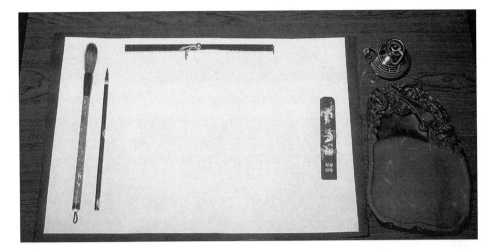

FIG. 16. Tools for painting: medium brush, small brush, paper-weight (at top), inkstick, ink stone, and small water pitcher. An absorbent felt mat has been placed beneath the paper.

not artificial, stone if possible, as it will produce ink more easily and absorb the ink into itself less quickly.

INK STICK

An ink (sumi) stick, which looks like a dark, dull block of wood, produces the ink you will use to paint when rubbed with water on the upper surface of the ink stone. You get what you pay for. Some sticks produce slightly different shades of ink. This may be indicated on the package or stick itself, but it is often written in Japanese or Chinese, so ask the clerk if you are not able to read the package. Most sumi sticks do offer fairly similar degrees of darkness of ink, so you need not worry too much about this point. Chinese ink sticks tend to be harder than their Japanese counterparts and may thus require more grinding time. Liquid inks are also available.

PAPER

Paper is, like ink stones, quite variable in regard to price and quality, but finding variety is difficult outside of Asia. While even rough newsprint can be used effectively, try to find paper designed for sumi-e and shodo. Yasutomo and Company makes a good tablet of sumi-e paper, as well as acceptable liquid ink. The stores listed in the section beginning on page 139 are also worth contacting.

Your work can be mounted when it is finished. First, a backing paper is added to take out any wrinkles, and the work is then mounted to form a hanging scroll. This is an expensive process that is best left to a professional. As an alternative, you can purchase thick, stiff, pre-mounted pieces of paper called *shikishi* and *tanzaku*. (See Figure 17.) Both are fairly inexpensive. Shikishi are roughly eight inches wide and seven inches high, while tanzaku are usually just over two inches wide and one foot, two inches long. You can also buy commercially produced universal frames for these paper types because shikishi and tanzaku are uniformly sized.

OTHER MATERIALS

Serious calligraphers also often use a small brush rest (for when they are not holding an ink-covered brush); a water dropper, such as an eyedropper or small water pitcher (for adding water to the ink stone); and a felt mat *(shitajiki)* to absorb ink that may bleed through the paper. Of these last few items, the only one that is really needed is some sort of material to protect the surface of your table. For novices, several sheets of newspaper, placed under the painting/calligraphy paper, will suffice.

FIG. 17. Stiff, premounted paper for painting works intended for display. Shikishi paper is about 8 x 7 inches. Tanzaku paper is about 2 x 14 inches. Frames are available in both sizes.

Beginning to Paint

Arrange your paper squarely in front of you, on a level table that is not too high. You may want to sit on a cushion, as this is easier than trying to adjust the height of your table. If you own a low table, the *seiza* posture is recommended (see pages 84–85).

Control the top portion of the paper with your paperweight and the bottom section with your left hand. The work that is to be copied can be placed either above or to the left of your paper, and your ink stone rests off to the right side of the paper. Sumi-e and shodo paper often has a rough side and a smooth side. If the rough side is used, it is easier to produce a dry brush effect in which white paper shows through the ink *(kasure)*, which is desirable in some cases. Kobara Ran-

107

seki Sensei feels that using the rough side of the paper is advisable for many students because it is less slippery, and consequently brush control is more easily maintained.

As you paint, you can adjust the positions of some of the items before you, especially the paper, but avoid tipping and tilting your paper at angles because this makes it more difficult to achieve balance in the artwork. Hold your brush in your right hand, and make a point of adopting a posture in which the mind and body are united.

GRINDING THE INK

Fill the receptacle portion of the ink stone with either liquid ink or, more traditionally, cool water. Fill it completely if you will be painting for some time, or just add a bit if you are only going to paint for a limited period. If you're using water, grasp your ink stick in your right hand, dip into the water reservoir in the stone, and draw some of the water onto the flat surface of the stone. Using moderate-sized oval motions, gently grind the end of your ink stick against the flat part of the stone's surface. In time, ink is produced, and the more you grind, the darker the ink will become. You do not need to always try to convert the water in the reservoir into ink. (This is possible, but time-consuming.) As the ink starts to run out, bring up some more water from the reservoir and grind a little more to make the color consistent. Ink color can be tested on another sheet of paper prior to painting.

USING THE BRUSH

A new brush needs to be soaked in water to remove the stiffening agent that holds the bristles together. Gently massaging the brush hair can speed up this process. Some authorities suggest that beginners leave this stiffening agent in the small brush because the small brush is used to paint fine lines.

Before covering the brush with ink, wet the bristles of the brush thoroughly and then gently squeeze the water out, forming a sharp tip with your fingers. (This helps hold the brush hairs together.) Using the tip of the brush, draw some ink onto the flat surface of the ink stone and wipe it over the entire surface of the brush hairs so that the bristles are completely covered with ink. It takes experience to learn how much ink to use in coating the brush. If you wish to produce a bleeding effect *(nijimi)*, the brush is somewhat oversaturated with sumi. On the other hand, if you are aiming for the kasure dry-brush effect, you should use an undersaturated brush.

As you paint, the brush hairs may split, but they can always be formed back into a point by smoothing them against the flat ink stone surface. Be careful not to add too much additional ink while doing this.

When painting practice is finished, thoroughly clean your brush and ink stone using cool water and no soap. Squeeze the water from your brush and always form the hair back into a point. (Strangely, a fairly large number of people have arrived at the mistaken notion that the ink stone is never washed. This is false. Failing to wash your suzuri eventually ruins it and only helps to financially support ink stone manufacturers.)

To clean a brush from which the stiffening agent has not been removed, rinse it under water briefly and then wipe it repeatedly against a clean paper towel. Always wipe in the same direction by pulling the brush toward you, not by pushing the bristles away from you.

Exercise One: Controlling Brush Pressure and Line Thickness

Hold the brush stem so that it is roughly perpendicular to the paper. Although the brush will tilt as you paint, the fundamental position of the stem is vertical. Control the thickness of line not by inclining the brush but by pressing down and raising up. Downward pressure will produce a thicker line, and lifting up to use the very tip of the bristles will produce a fine line.

Painting in a smooth, continuous fashion from left to right, try copying the line shown in Figure 18. You may require several attempts to produce a smooth transition from thickness to thinness and back again.

To control the thickness of line, you must be able to control your mind and body. The principles of mental and physical harmony that have been outlined in the preceding chapters contain many of the essential points for achieving such a state of mind-body mastery.

Exercise Two: The Three Essential Brush Strokes

Three brush strokes are introduced to novices studying Kobara Ranseki's system of shodo. They are utilized to learn *daho* (pressing method), *nenpo* (twisting method), and *zoho* (overlapping method). The following exercises do not necessarily represent the most common brush strokes found in shodo, but they will teach you the most about how to control your brush. Because the mind moves the brush, these exercises allow you to train your mind as well as your ability to coordinate the body and mind.

FIG. 18. Try painting a smooth transition, left to right, from thick to thin and back again.

DAHO

You study daho by learning to make a dot, as in Figure 19. Try copying this dot by pressing downward while holding the brush perpendicular to the paper. Your brush is lowered onto the paper at an angle, and downward pressure is applied to somewhat flatten the bristles. As you press down, draw the brush slightly toward the bottom of the paper and lift up as you draw the tip of the brush back to the center of your dot. A small semicircle is drawn, in conjunction with downward pressure, to form a dot.

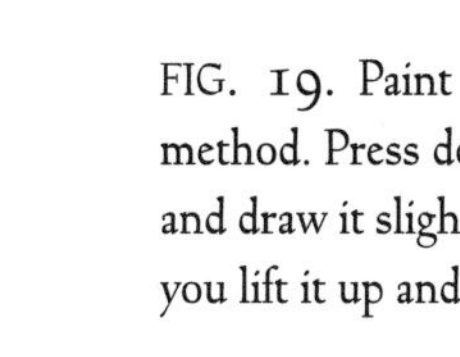

FIG. 19. Paint a dot to study daho, the pressing method. Press downward on the perpendicular brush and draw it slightly toward the bottom of the paper as you lift it up and bring the tip back to the center.

NENPO

In nenpo, you touch the paper using just the tip of the brush hairs and delicate downward pressure. (See Figure 20.) Twist the brush in the opposite direction as you continue to move it toward the bottom of the paper, and press down as in daho to form the rest of the brush stroke. (See Figure 21.) The brush starts off pointing to the upper right, twists downward to use the body of the bristles, lifts, and then the tip trails off slightly to the left. Nenpo is, more or less, daho with a gentle S-shaped curve. Although Figures 20 and 21 show nenpo in two stages, the stroke is drawn with one continuous movement of varying pressure.

FIG. 20. For nenpo, the twisting method, you begin by touching the paper using just the tip of the brush hairs and delicate downward pressure.

FIG. 21. Continue the nenpo stroke by twisting the brush in the opposite direction as you continue to move it toward the bottom of the paper; then press down as in daho to form the rest of the stroke.

ZOHO

To study zoho, begin by moving the tip of the brush lightly from right to left. (See Figure 22.). Then, go back over this thin line from left to right. (See Figure 23.) As you move the brush from left to right, apply gentle but gradually increasing pressure to thicken the line. At the end of the line, let the brush lift so that only the tip is touching again. Allow the pressure to trail off so that a fine point is formed at the end and the flow of ki continues to the right as your brush leaves the paper. Zoho involves a single continuous motion that flows briefly from right to left, and then from left to right.

FIG. 22. To study zoho, the overlapping method, begin by moving the tip of the brush lightly from right to left.

FIG. 23. Then, to finish the zoho stroke, go back over the stroke in Figure 22 from left to right, increasing pressure to thicken the line in the center and then reducing pressure so that the a fine point is formed at the right. The flow of ki continues as your brush leaves the paper.

FIG. 24. Writing the top of the character character *chu* involves nenpo (at top), daho (the left stroke of the "roof"), and a modified zoho stroke that flicks back to the left (from the right edge of the "roof"). The remaining strokes are written with varying brush pressures to create a rhythmic range of thick and thin lines.

COMBINING THE THREE BASIC STROKES

Finally, you can try painting the character *chu* (heaven), which uses all three brush strokes to form the top component, or radical. (See Figure 24.) Paint nenpo first, then daho on the left, followed by a horizontal variation of zoho that makes use of a returning flick of the brush from right to left. Then try the remaining strokes.

Exercise Three: *Kaisho, Gyosho, and Sosho*

The three most common script styles found in Japanese calligraphy are: kaisho (Figure 25), which is the equivalent of printing in English; gyosho (Figure 26), which is similar to semicursive writing; and sosho (Figure 27), which is equivalent to cursive English handwriting. Each illustration features the character *kokoro*, meaning "heart" or "soul," painted three different ways.

Each of these different scripts projects a different feeling, and each requires a unique state of mind. Studying kaisho, gyosho, and sosho allows you to understand and master divergent mental states. Try writing these three variants.

KAISHO

When using kaisho script, you will most clearly show the structure of the character. Note that the ends of certain strokes are tapered, and should have an almost organic appearance not unlike bamboo leaves and stems. Printed-style characters need a firm, but not stiff,

FIG. 25. *Kokoro* written in kaisho. This shows the clear structure of the character. Ends of strokes are tapered, and inside each stroke is a definite central line that represents the movement of the center of the brush bristles, effectively a line of ki.

FIG. 26. *Kokoro* written in gyosho. This offers a strong sensation of visual rhythm made up of upward and downward pressure combined with thick and thin strokes. Gyosho rhythms
are good for assessing mental tension and composure.

demeanor. Inside each brush stroke is a central line. This personifies
the movement of the center of the bristles and it must be kept steady. It
is actually more of a mental line—a line of ki. This ki line must be
drawn decisively in your mind. Rigidly trying to hold the hand steady is
not the answer because this will only create lifeless characters.

GYOSHO

While kaisho makes use of a superlative command of space,
gyosho offers a strong sensation of visual rhythm. Rhythm is destroyed
by tension, and semicursive-style characters will reveal when you are

tightening your body and losing composure. In gyosho, it is acceptable to run some strokes together, and although in this case the word "heart" is painted in one continuous stroke, rhythm is still present. It is a rhythm of upward and downward pressure combined with thickness and thinness of line.

SOSHO

Cursive-style characters are painted with an even greater sense of an unbroken flow of ki. They tend to be rather abstract, and most Japanese cannot read them unless they are studying shodo. Think of sosho

FIG. 27. *Kokoro* written in sosho. This cursive, more abstract style displays an unbroken sense of ki. It looks effortless but in fact is controlled by vigorous practice and a firm understanding of the character's underlying structure.

as being more abbreviated and quickly written than semicursive-style characters. While cursive style appears to exhibit an effortless quality, you should be careful not to totally lose the sense of structure that was developed in your study of printed-style symbols. For this reason, students learn kaisho before practicing cursive-style kanji. Sosho contains the structure of printed-style and the rhythm of semicursive characters, which are combined to create a script that flows like dynamically rushing water.

Composition One: The Enso

Originating in Zen, the enso at first glance may appear to be nothing more than a circle. (See Figure 28.) Yet when painted in a state of mind-body unification by a skilled artist, it is filled with ki and becomes a circle of infinity. The enso is not a Japanese character, but more a form of abstract art used to convey that which is beyond words.

Try painting an enso, circling from left to right, to get a visual representation of your mental and physical state at the moment.

While turning your wrist, press down strongly as in Figure 29. Note that in Figure 30 the wrist and arm have twisted the other way as the circle is formed, and pressure decreases to form a tapered point at the end. Your hand must not stop abruptly at this point but should gradually lift while the flow of ki continues through space in the same direction it was traveling. In other words, follow through mentally and physically.

Note that the enso began from a point of stillness, transformed itself into a dynamic, almost violent motion, and finally gathered all of its energy into a still and infinitely decreasing point at the end. The

FIG. 28. Composition One. The enso, when painted in a
state of mind-body unification, becomes a circle of infinity.

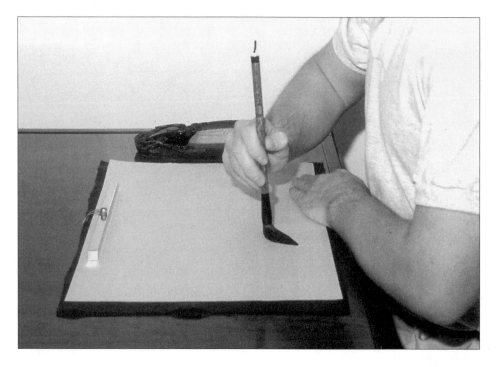

FIG. 29. To begin the enso, press down
strongly while turning your wrist.

enso expresses the essential oneness of opposites and acts as a depic-
tion of the unity of all aspects of nature.

Your *inkan* (seal) that contains the characters for your name can
be placed in the space between the beginning and ending of your brush
stroke. Placement of the seal can have a dramatic effect on the balance
of your work, because it is the only spot of color in a monochromatic
field. Asian name seals and traditional red seal ink can be purchased
through the sources listed on pages 139–40.

Alternately, your name can be signed to the left of your work and
followed by the inkan.

Because your body reflects your mind, the painting of an enso is an

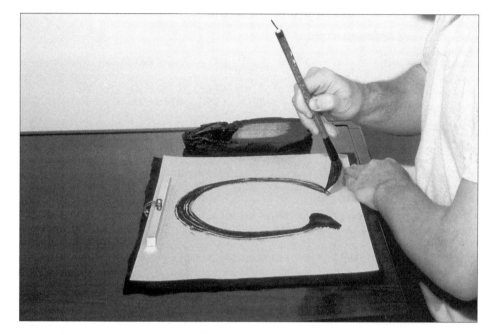

FIG. 30. To finish the enso, twist the wrist and arm the other way as the circle is formed; then decrease pressure to form a tapered point at the end.

opportunity to see yourself more clearly by noticing the relationship between your attitude and the enso itself.

Composition Two: The Coin

Composition Two is an abstract painting of an Asian coin, complete with the square hole in the center. (See Figure 31.) At the celebrated Ryoanji Zen temple in Kyoto is an ancient well in the shape of this coin, with the water resting in the coin's square center. This image makes use of the famed Zen enso again, and the four characters on the coin read:

Ware tada taru o shiru.
The only thing I know is that I'm perfectly satisfied.

This design is unique and clever. It is composed of four kanji, each of which has an identical square component. These characters are read in a clockwise manner, following the motion of the enso. They are arranged so that they all share the square radical, which also serves as the center hole of the coin. These kanji are:

> *ware* (I, oneself); see Figure 32
> *tada* (only, perfectly); see Figure 33
> *taru* (be satisfied); see Figure 34
> *shiru* (to know); see Figure 35

Start by copying and practicing these characters before attempting to reproduce the complete painting.

Now, to try recreating this image, first paint an enso (Figure 36).

Next, paint the square center of the coin (Figure 37). It is also possible to write the entire kanji *ware* at this point, followed by the other three components.

Add the top of the first kanji (Figure 38), followed by the right side of the second character (Figure 39), then the bottom of the third symbol (Figure 40), and, finally, the left side of the fourth kanji (Figure 41). Your seal can be placed in the same spot as in Composition 1.

The kanji in the actual composition have strokes that are slightly more connected than in Figures 32–35, for a more dynamic feeling.

FIG. 31. Composition Two. Abstract painting of an Asian coin, complete with the square hole in the center that forms a part of the four characters arranged around it.

FIG. 32. *Ware* (I, oneself).

FIG. 33. *Tada* (only, perfectly).

FIG. 34. *Taru* (be satisfied).

FIG. 35. *Shiru* (to know).

FIG. 36. To draw the coin, begin with an enso, as in Composition 1.

FIG. 37. Paint the square center of the coin.

FIG. 38. Paint the top of the first kanji.

FIG. 39. Paint the right side of the second character. The second component is written in one continuous stroke

129

FIG. 40. Paint the bottom of the third symbol.

FIG. 41. Paint the left side of the fourth kanji.

Composition Three: A Bonfire and a Poem

Your final composition contains an abstract painting of a bonfire, logs, and scattered leaves, along with a haiku poem. The work in Figure 42 was painted by Ohsaki Jun, my student. The poem reads:

Taku hodo wa
Kaze ga motekuru
Ochiba kana.

Building bonfires
Wind currents are bringing
Falling leaves.

This haiku suggests the perfect harmony that pervades all of the universe. It is written in connected cursive-style and features the use of kanji, kana (Japanese phonetic symbols), and hentaigana (archaic Chinese characters used phonetically). See Figure 43.

Start off by painting the bonfire. Turn your wrist as in the photo in Figure 44. At this point, press down strongly, then twist the brush around and up, causing the brush hairs to separate.

Move the brush upward in a wavering line with an undulating up-down action to create smoke as in Figure 45. (Use a fairly dry brush for this effect.)

Now, making use of the split brush hairs, add the logs and burning debris by drawing wide left-to-right diagonal brush strokes. Form a point out of the bristles again and lightly dab the brush tip around the base of the bonfire, in a random pattern, to create leaves.

Last, using your small brush, write the haiku in smooth, contin-

FIG. 42. Composition Three. Abstract painting of a bonfire, logs, and scattered leaves, with a haiku poem. Painting by Ohsaki Jun.

焚くほどは
風がもて
くる
おちばかな

FIG. 43. Detail of the poem in FIG. 42: *Taku hodo wa / Kaze ga motekuru / Ochiba kana*. The poem is written in a mix of kanji, kana, and hentaigana. The same poem is also shown here in standard printed characters

FIG. 44. Turn your wrist as shown to begin the bonfire stroke.

uous lines, moving from top to bottom and from right to left. Note in Figure 46 that the left hand (or wrist) can be used as a light support for the right wrist. Because it is easy for the hand to wobble when it's writing small characters, calligraphers often gently slide the right wrist along the back of the left hand or wrist as they paint down the paper.

Apply ink to the brush at the beginning of the first line of characters on the right. Let the ink gradually run out to create a lighter and drier second line.

Then, apply more ink for the third line, so that the first line is dark, the second line is light, and the third line is dark. This alternation of tone is known as *no-tan* (light-dark), and it is vital for creating a sense of variety and rhythm in your work.

Once the haiku is finished, your seal can be placed between the bonfire and the poem.

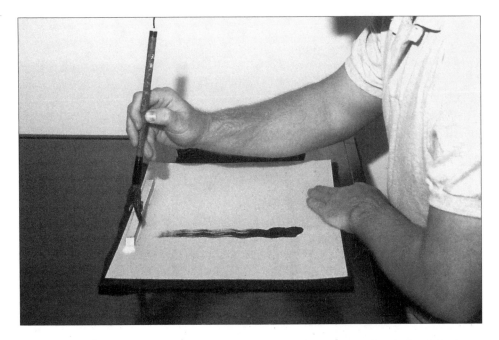

FIG. 45. Twist the brush around and up so that the brush hairs separate. Move the brush upward in a wavering line to create smoke.

Painting kana with the small brush requires a different use of the
mind and body than that required by a larger brush (although the principles of brush control are the same). Try to note how the use of the
small brush relates to the larger brush. If you find this composition difficult, go back to the basic concepts of mind-body-brush unification
that have already been outlined. These concepts do not change regardless of what you may be holding in your hand.

What Next?

Shodo has been used in this book primarily as a single representation of the Japanese "do" and as a means of exploring meditation in

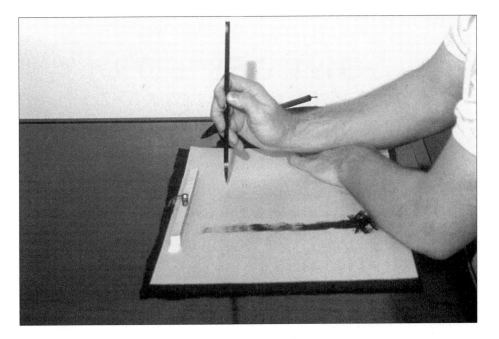

FIG. 46. When writing the haiku, use the left hand or wrist as a light support for your right wrist as you work.

action. If you'd like to pursue shodo further, find yourself a good teacher (see the section beginning on page 138 for some advice on how to proceed). But even if you don't pursue formal shodo instruction, I hope *Brush Meditation* has given you a better understanding of Japanese cultural arts and how they can serve as meditative activities. The principles of harmony outlined in the preceding pages are more than just a means to success in shodo. They relate to the minds and bodies of people everywhere. You can thus use the topics outlined in this book to enhance many aspects of your daily life. I especially hope they will prompt you to look at the genuine characteristics of your self and its relationship to nature and, in this way, directly discover the true nature of your existence.

SOURCES FOR INSTRUCTION & SUPPLIES

All genuine understanding of the topics in this book must be arrived at through actual experience. This was the main reason for including a sampling of exercises and compositions for you to experiment with in Chapter 4. If, after reading this book and trying its exercises, you would like to proceed further, you may wish to find a qualified teacher. Or, you may need information on where to purchase art supplies like brushes, ink, ink stones, and paper. The following information should help.

How Do I Find an Instructor?

This, in many ways, is the most important question for any prospective student of the Japanese cultural arts. A competent teacher is indispensable, although some publications can serve as an introduction to a given art, offer material for contemplation, or function as an effective supplement to hands-on training.

I offer instruction in Japanese yoga and fine arts. Please contact me if you have questions or comments about the material in this book. Write or email to:

The Sennin Foundation Center
for Japanese Cultural Arts
P. O. Box 5447
Richmond, CA 94805
HEDavey@aol.com

You can also find more information on the Sennin Foundation Web Site at:

www.michionline.org/sennin-center/

Another good resource is Michi Online: Journal of the Japanese Cultural Arts:

www.michionline.org

If you live outside of my immediate vicinity, a local instructor will be necessary. You'll probably have better luck finding a sumi-e teacher than a shodo teacher, but some instructors are competent in both arts. Here are some simple ways of locating a teacher:

- If a Japanese community center is nearby, try checking on their various classes. They may offer the kind of instruction mentioned in this text.

• Local colleges may have classes in Japanese calligraphy or painting.

• Many Buddhist churches and centers offer classes in Asian cultural arts. Look in the telephone directory for a nearby Buddhist church.

• Try contacting the nearest Japanese consulate and asking for assistance.

• If none of the above resources can point you to the kind of teacher you are looking for, try talking to instructors of other Japanese art forms such as judo or tea ceremony. These teachers may know of someone that can help you.

• In general, make a point of getting involved in the local Japanese-American community, as this will enhance your understanding of all the Japanese arts. It can also open many doors.

Finding a qualified teacher is never quick and easy. I looked for several years before discovering an exceptional instructor. Once you have a teacher, be prepared to spend a sizable amount

of time and effort in studying. While this may seem a bit daunting to the beginner, it is vital to realize that the rewards are definitely equal to the energy expended.

Where Can I Buy Supplies?

The first place to check for shodo supplies is your nearest art supply store. Shodo and sumi-e both use the same sort of brush, paper, ink stone, and ink, so be sure to let the clerk know this. Bear in mind, however, that while you may get a good price at the local art supply shop, you will rarely find a good selection or tools of good quality.

For a fine selection of supplies of varying quality, the New Unique Company in San Francisco's Chinatown is excellent. Brushes, name seals, paper, and ink stones can all be purchased here. The owner sells equipment for Chinese calligraphy and painting, but most materials are the same as those used in Japan. Write or call for more information:

The New Unique Company
838 Grant Street
San Francisco, CA 94108
(415) 981-2036

The Kinokuniya Bookstores of America chain carries art supplies at some of its locations. (They are primarily booksellers and can help you find additional written information about the Japanese fine arts.) They can sometimes offer suggestions about finding a teacher. Stores are located throughout the U.S. at:

Kinokuniya San Francisco
1581 Webster Street
San Francisco, CA 94115
(415) 567-7625

Kinokuniya San Jose
675 Saratoga Avenue
San Jose, CA 95129
(408)252-1300

Kinokuniya Los Angeles
123 Ellison S. Onizuka Street
Los Angeles, CA 90012
(213) 687-4447

Kinokuniya Costa Mesa
665 Paularino Avenue
Costa Mesa, CA 92626
(714) 434-9986

Kinokuniya Seattle
519 6th Avenue
Seattle, WA 98104
(206) 587-2477

Kinokuniya New York
10 West 49th Street
New York, NY 10020
(212) 765-7766

Kinokuniya New Jersey
595 River Road
Edgewater, NJ 07020
(201) 941-7580

Kinokuniya Portland
10500 SW Beaverton-Hillsdale Highway
Beaverton, OR 97005
(503) 641-6240

Other stores in North America that sell ink, brushes, and paper are:

Aiko's Art Materials
3347 North Clark Street
Chicago, IL 60657
(773) 404-5600

M. Flax
10852 Lindbrook Drive
Los Angeles, CA 90024
(310) 208-3529

Pearl Paint
308 Canal Street
New York, NY 10013
(800) 221-6845

Ichiyo Art Center
432 East Paces Ferry Road
Atlanta, GA 30305
(404) 233-1846

Five Eggs
213 West San Francisco Street
Santa Fe, NM 87501
(505) 986-3403

A wholesaler that can direct you to a store in your local area is:

Yasutomo and Company
490 Eccles Avenue
South San Francisco, CA 94080
(650) 737-8888

NOTES

1. Library of Congress and Yomiuri Shinbun, *Words in Motion: Modern Japanese Calligraphy* (Tokyo: Library of Congress and Yomiuri Shinbun, 1984), p. 44.

2. Leonard Koren, *Wabi-Sabi: for Artists, Designers, Poets & Philosophers* (Berkeley: Stone Bridge Press, 1994), pp. 40–41.

3. H. E. Davey, *The Way of the Universe* (Albany, Calif.: Sennin Organization, 1985), pp. 66–67.

4. Ibid., p. 80.

5. John Stevens, *The Sword of No-Sword: Life of the Master Warrior Tesshu* (Boulder, Colo.: Shambhala, 1984), p. 142.

6. Library of Congress and Yomiuri Shinbun, *Words in Motion*, p. 41.

7. Nakamura Tempu and Hashimoto Tetsuichi, *Ways for Unification of Mind and Body* (Tokyo: n.pub., n.d.), p. 7.

8. Michel Random, *Japan: Strategy of the Unseen* (Northamptonshire, England: Crucible, 1987), pp. 192–93.

9. Trevor P. Leggett, *Zen and the Ways* (London: Routledge and Kegan Paul, 1978), p. 197.

10. Random, *Japan*, p. 190.

11. Omori Sogen and Terayama Katsujo, *Zen and the Art of Calligraphy: The Essence of Sho* (London: Routledge and Kegan Paul, 1983), p. 10.

12. Trevor P. Leggett, *First Zen Reader* (Rutland, Vt., and Tokyo: Tuttle, 1960), p. 224.

13. Kobara Ranseki, *The Spirit of the Brush Favors No Nation*, trans. H. E. Davey (Tokyo: Nihon Keizai Shinbun, 1988).

14. Haruo Yamaoka, *Meditation Gut Enlightenment: The Way of Hara* (South San Francisco: Heian International, 1976), p. 69.

15. Richard Heckler, *The Anatomy of Change* (Boulder, Colo.: Shambhala, 1984), pp. 82–84.

16. Random, *Japan*, p. 190.

GLOSSARY

bokuju: liquid ink

budo: "the martial ways"

bun-chin: paperweight

chado: "the way of tea," tea ceremony

chu-fude: medium-sized brush

daho: "pressing method," a technique of manipulating the brush

do: "the way," used to describe a Japanese art that is practiced as a means of spiritual realization

enso: the painted ink circle of Zen

fude: brush

fudoshin: "immovable mind," a state of spiritual and physical stability

gyosho: semicursive-style script

hara: "abdomen," a natural center in the lower abdomen used as a point of concentration in various meditative disciplines and Japanese arts

hentaigana: also "man'yogana," an antiquated script that uses Chinese characters phonetically

hiragana: cursive Japanese syllabary

inkan: Japanese seal or stamp

kado: "the way of flowers," flower arrangement

kaisho: printed-style script

kana: Japanese syllabaries

kanji: Chinese characters

kasure: dry brush strokes

katakana: angular Japanese syllabary

ki: life energy

ko-fude: small brush

nenpo: "twisting method," a technique of manipulating the brush

nijimi: wet, bleeding brush strokes

no-tan: writing with alternatingly light and dark ink

sabi: elegant simplicity, an antique appearance

seiza: Japanese kneeling posture

sensei: teacher

shibui: elegant

shibumi: elegance

Shin-shin-toitsu-do: "the way of mind and body unification," a form of Japanese yoga

shitajiki: felt undercloth for absorbing ink

sumi: ink, ink stick

sumi-e: ink painting

suzuri: ink stone

wabi: unpretentious, simple refinement

zoho: "overlapping method," a technique of manipulating the brush

AFTERWORD

My Japanese and American friends often wonder how a Caucasian, with only mediocre Japanese speaking ability, came to teach Japanese calligraphy and painting. They may be equally mystified that I've written about a subject rooted in Japanese language and sometimes thought of, by Japanese and Westerners alike, as being impenetrable to non-Japanese.

Nothing could be further from the truth. The path leading to this book supports my assertion that it's possible for people of other cultures to achieve success in shodo or any Japanese "do" form. In 1926, my late father was among the first non-Japanese to study Japanese martial arts, earning black belts in more than one discipline. At five years old, I was practicing aiki-jujutsu with him. Later, I began Shin-shin-toitsu-do style Japanese yoga and Japanese healing arts. By 1981, I was the Director of the Sennin Foundation Center for Japanese Cultural Arts, which offers instruction in Japanese yoga, healing arts, shodo, and martial arts.

As a boy, I was encouraged to paint, and due to martial arts training, I was exposed to Japanese calligraphy. I was an art major and sustained an interest in shodo and sumi-e, but to little avail. No teachers were accessible. In 1986, I met Kobara Ranseki Sensei, a master calligrapher/painter from Kyoto. Kobara Sensei, having received innumerable awards in shodo, including one from the Prime Minister of Japan, does not advertise for students. Because most of his pupils were from Japan, he taught in Japanese. Because he'd never attempted to instruct an American not fluent in Japanese, Mr. Kobara was none too sure about teaching me. Still, like a cliché from a bad movie, I kept coming back.

Since studying with Kobara Sensei, my Japanese has improved, and I've advanced in ranking and received various awards that substantiate shodo proficiency. I mention this only to support my assertion that it's indeed possible for people of other cultures to achieve success in shodo. Using shodo as an example, it's my intention to show the interrelationship between Japanese arts, as well as the way these skills, from flower arrangement to tea ceremony, can serve as meditations capable of enhancing the lives of everyone, regardless of nationality.

143

About the Author

H. E. Davey is the first non-Japanese to receive the title Shihan-Dai, the highest rank issued by Ranseki Sho Juku, an affiliate of Kokusai Shodo Bunka Koryu Kyokai, a worldwide Japanese calligraphy association. In 1988, his artwork was selected, out of several thousand submitted works, for exhibition at the International Shodo Exhibition in Urayasu, sponsored by the Japanese Ministry of Education and the Kokusai Shodo Bunka Koryu Kyokai. He received the Tokusen Award, the first non-Japanese to receive this honor. In subsequent years, his calligraphy and painting have been shown at this exhibit and received numerous awards, including the Jun Taisho, or the Associate Grand Prize, also a first for someone not of Japanese ancestry.

H. E. Davey is currently Director of the Sennin Foundation Center for Japanese Cultural Arts in the San Francisco Bay Area.

H. E. Davey and Kobara Ranseki Sensei in Japan at the 1989 International Shodo Exhibition.

 Also in the MICHI: JAPANESE ARTS AND WAYS series
The Japanese Way of the Flower: Ikebana as Moving Meditation
by H. E. Davey and Ann Kameoka

This second volume of "moving meditations" shows how simple Japanese flower arranging (ikebana) techniques can be used to refresh the body and restore the spirit. Emphasizing that ikebana is first and foremost a "Way"—a spiritual and meditative art—the book offers solid grounding in Japanese aesthetics and philosophy, with references to Zen, tea ceremony, and other traditional Japanese arts. Line drawings and color photographs show step-by-step arrangements especially for beginners and casual practitioners.

144 pp, 7 x 9", paper, 8 pp color, ISBN 1-880656-47-7, $16.95
Contact your bookseller or call Stone Bridge Press at 1-800-947-7271 • sbp@stonebridge.com